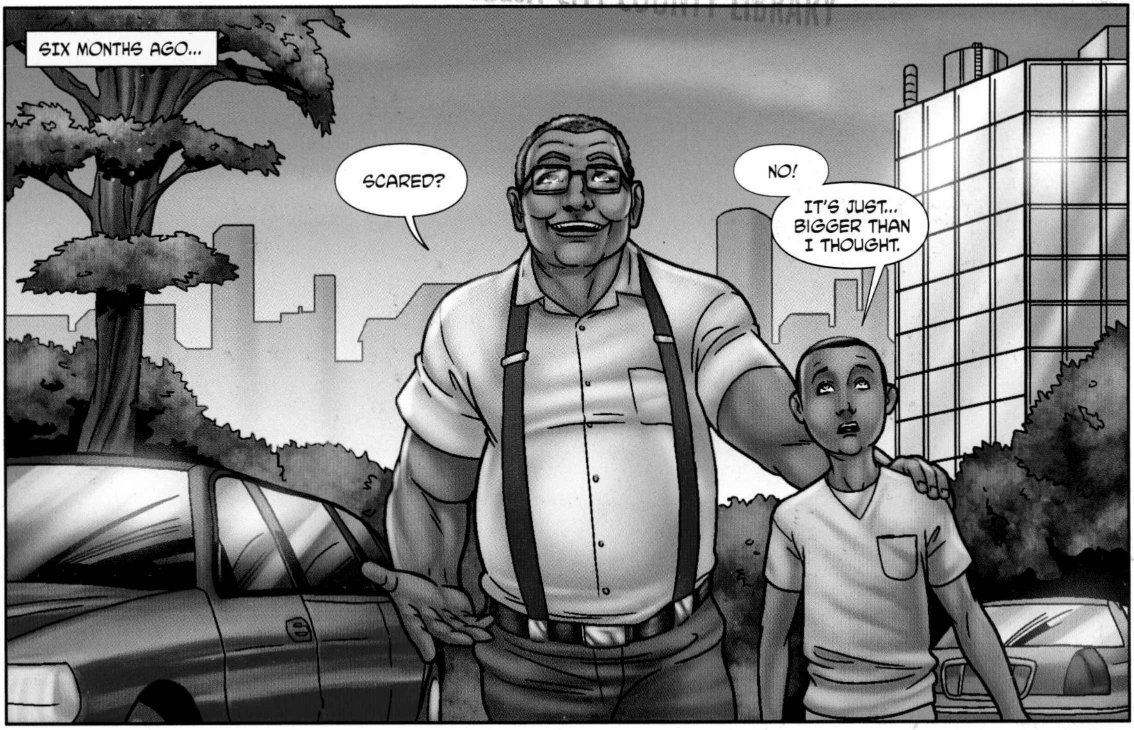
SIX MONTHS AGO...
SCARED?
NO!
IT'S JUST... BIGGER THAN I THOUGHT.

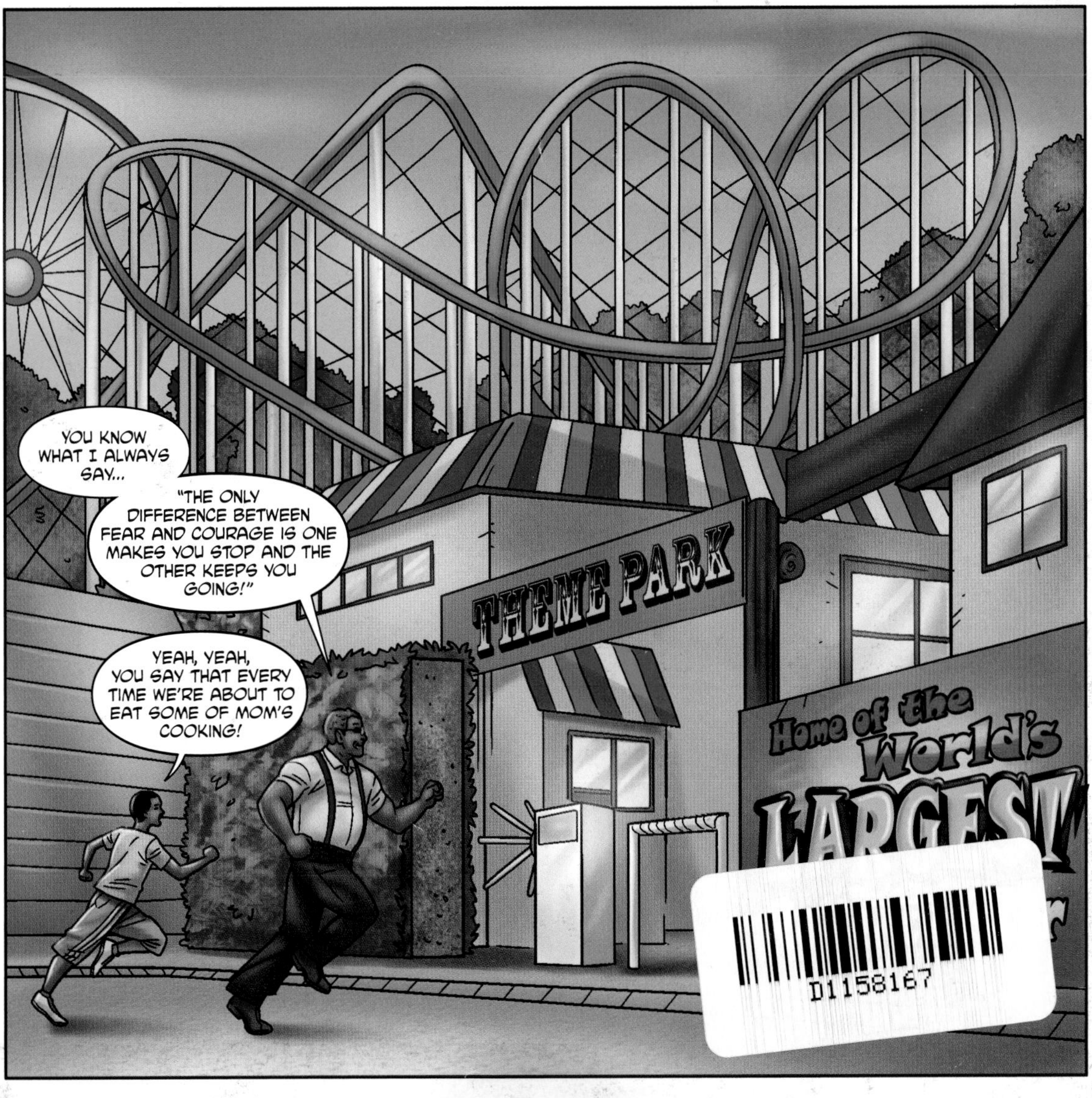
YOU KNOW WHAT I ALWAYS SAY...
"THE ONLY DIFFERENCE BETWEEN FEAR AND COURAGE IS ONE MAKES YOU STOP AND THE OTHER KEEPS YOU GOING!"
YEAH, YEAH, YOU SAY THAT EVERY TIME WE'RE ABOUT TO EAT SOME OF MOM'S COOKING!
THEME PARK
Home of the World's
LARGEST

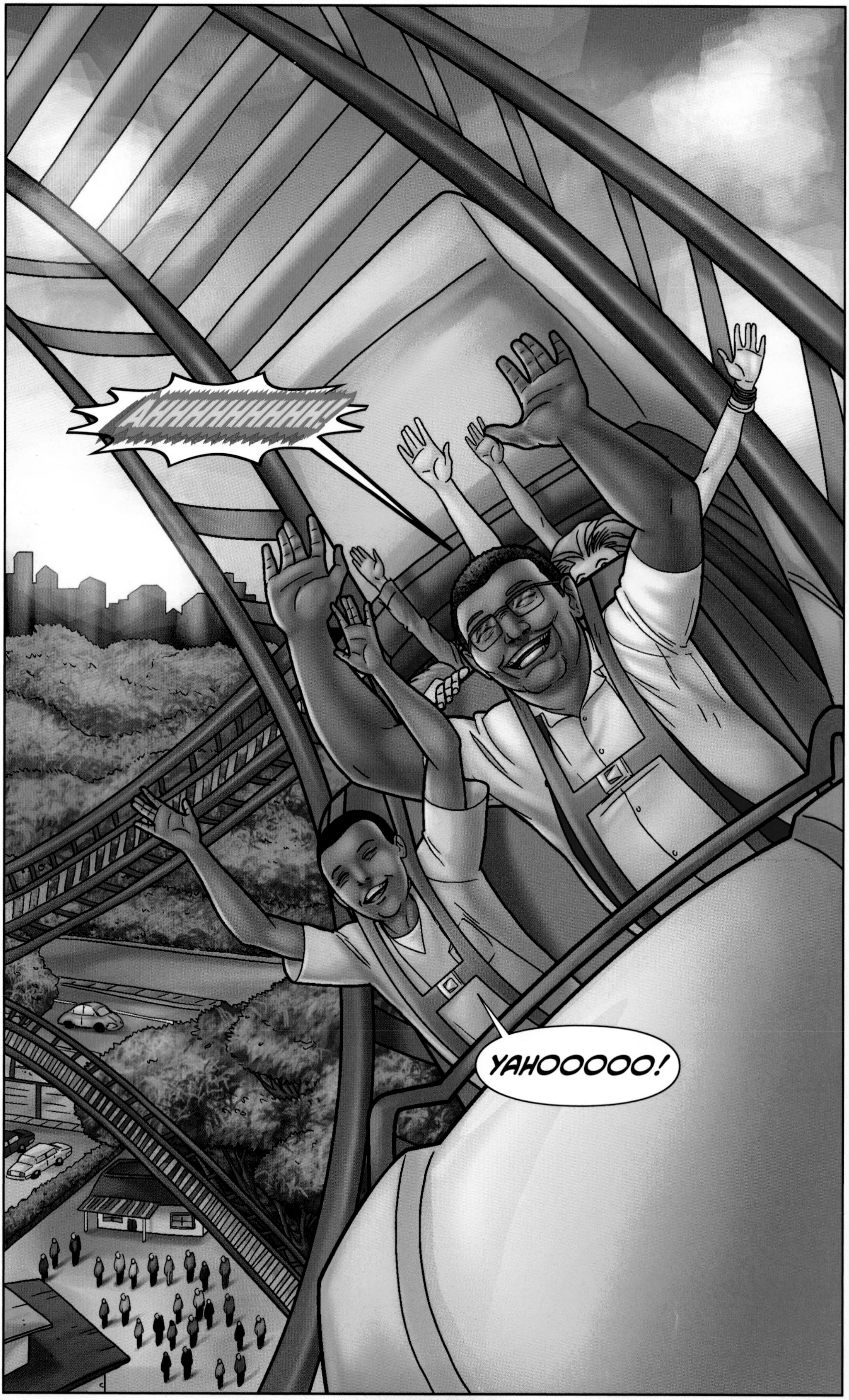
AHHHHHHHH!
YAHOOOOO!

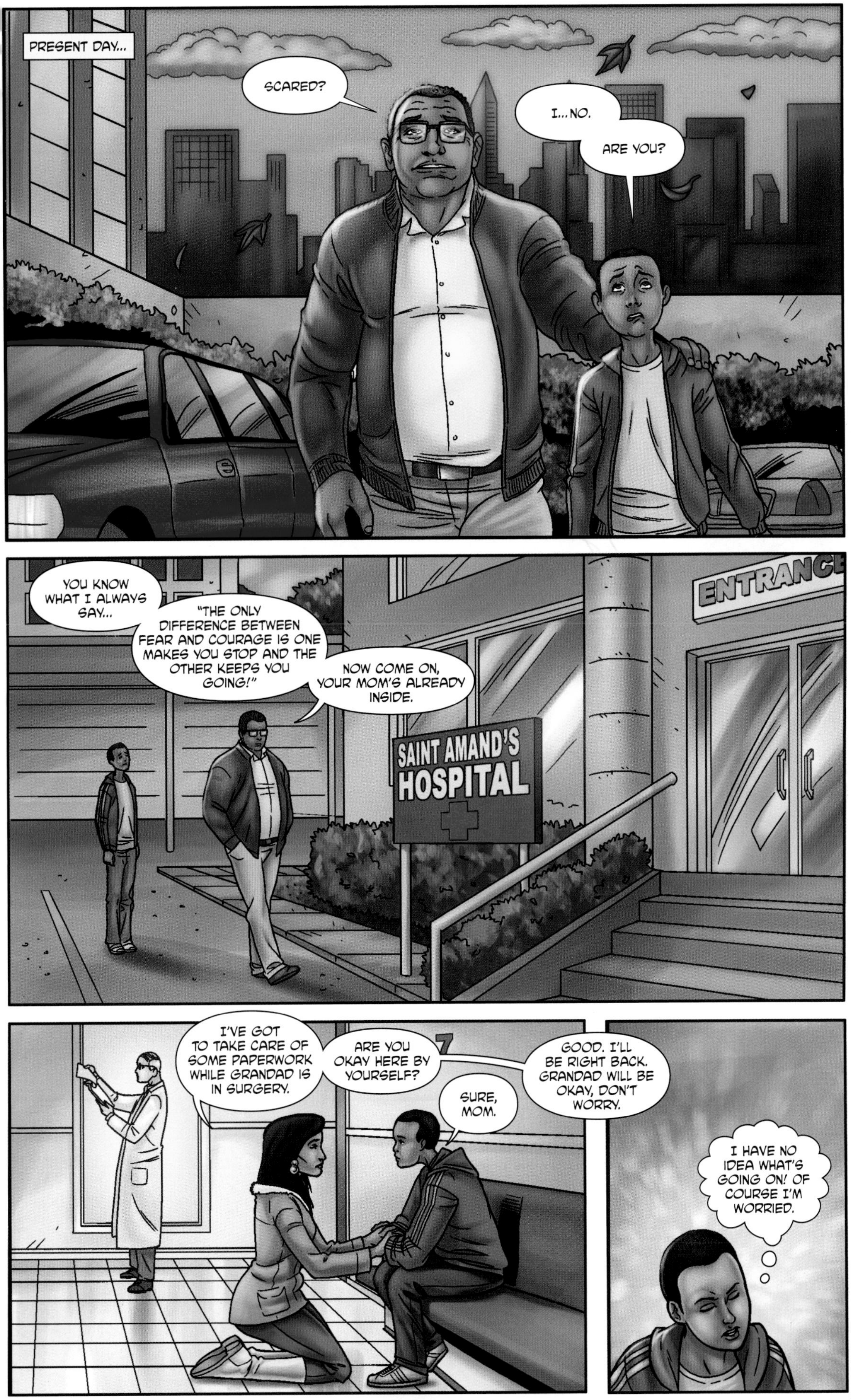
PRESENT DAY...
SCARED?
I...NO.
ARE YOU?
YOU KNOW WHAT I ALWAYS SAY...
"THE ONLY DIFFERENCE BETWEEN FEAR AND COURAGE IS ONE MAKES YOU STOP AND THE OTHER KEEPS YOU GOING!"
NOW COME ON, YOUR MOM'S ALREADY INSIDE.
ENTRANCE
SAINT AMAND'S HOSPITAL
I'VE GOT TO TAKE CARE OF SOME PAPERWORK WHILE GRANDAD IS IN SURGERY.
ARE YOU OKAY HERE BY YOURSELF?
SURE, MOM.
GOOD. I'LL BE RIGHT BACK. GRANDAD WILL BE OKAY, DON'T WORRY.
I HAVE NO IDEA WHAT'S GOING ON! OF COURSE I'M WORRIED.

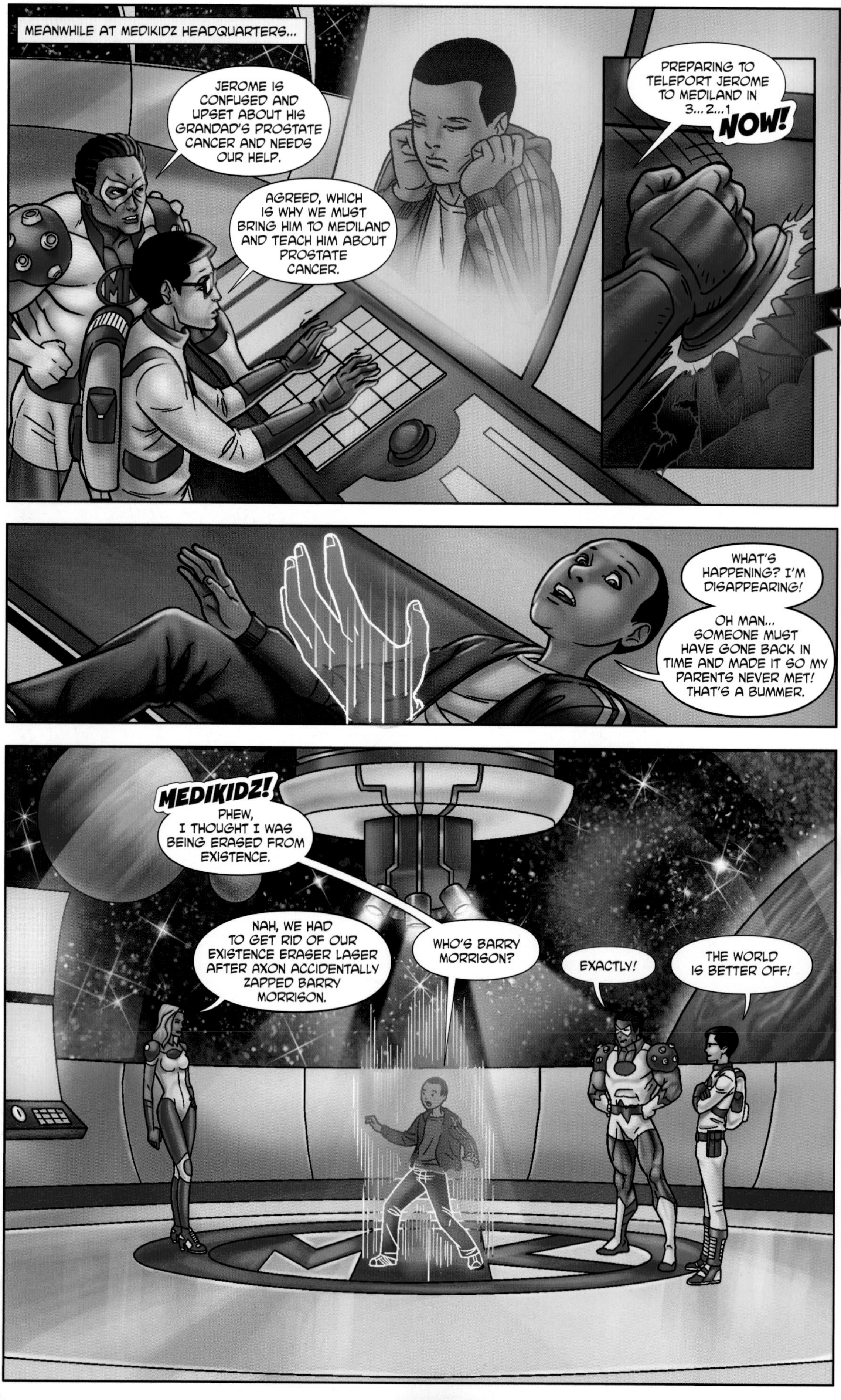
MEANWHILE AT MEDIKIDZ HEADQUARTERS...
JEROME IS CONFUSED AND UPSET ABOUT HIS GRANDAD'S PROSTATE CANCER AND NEEDS OUR HELP.
AGREED, WHICH IS WHY WE MUST BRING HIM TO MEDILAND AND TEACH HIM ABOUT PROSTATE CANCER.
PREPARING TO TELEPORT JEROME TO MEDILAND IN 3...2...1 NOW!
WHAT'S HAPPENING? I'M DISAPPEARING!
OH MAN... SOMEONE MUST HAVE GONE BACK IN TIME AND MADE IT SO MY PARENTS NEVER MET! THAT'S A BUMMER.
MEDIKIDZ! PHEW, I THOUGHT I WAS BEING ERASED FROM EXISTENCE.
NAH, WE HAD TO GET RID OF OUR EXISTENCE ERASER LASER AFTER AXON ACCIDENTALLY ZAPPED BARRY MORRISON.
WHO'S BARRY MORRISON?
EXACTLY!
THE WORLD IS BETTER OFF!

I KNOW IT MUST BE SCARY TO HEAR THAT SOMEONE YOU LOVE HAS PROSTATE CANCER, BUT WE'RE GOING TO HELP YOU UNDERSTAND EXACTLY WHAT THAT MEANS.

YOU COULD START BY EXPLAINING WHAT THE PROSTATE IS... AND WHAT THIS BUTTON DOES.

ACK! STOP THAT! ONE MORE BURP COULD SEND MEDILAND HEADQUARTERS HURTLING OFF INTO DEEP SPACE!

THE PROSTATE IS A SMALL GLAND THAT ONLY MEN HAVE.

YES! HAH! TAKE THAT, SKINDY! BOYS RULE!

THAT'S NOT NECESSARILY A GOOD THING IN THIS INSTANCE, GASTRO.

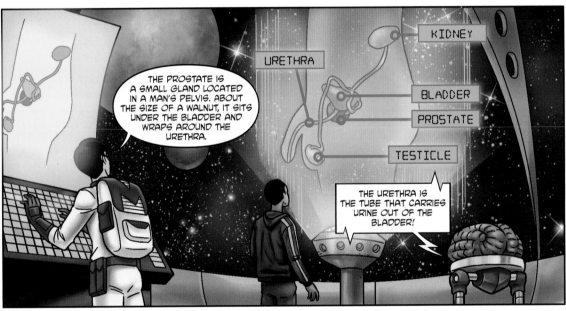

THE PROSTATE IS A SMALL GLAND LOCATED IN A MAN'S PELVIS. ABOUT THE SIZE OF A WALNUT, IT SITS UNDER THE BLADDER AND WRAPS AROUND THE URETHRA.

URETHRA

KIDNEY

BLADDER

PROSTATE

TESTICLE

THE URETHRA IS THE TUBE THAT CARRIES URINE OUT OF THE BLADDER!

MEDI-BRIDGE, TO THE PROSTATE! LET'S TAKE A CLOSER LOOK!

LAST ONE IN IS...ER...LAST!

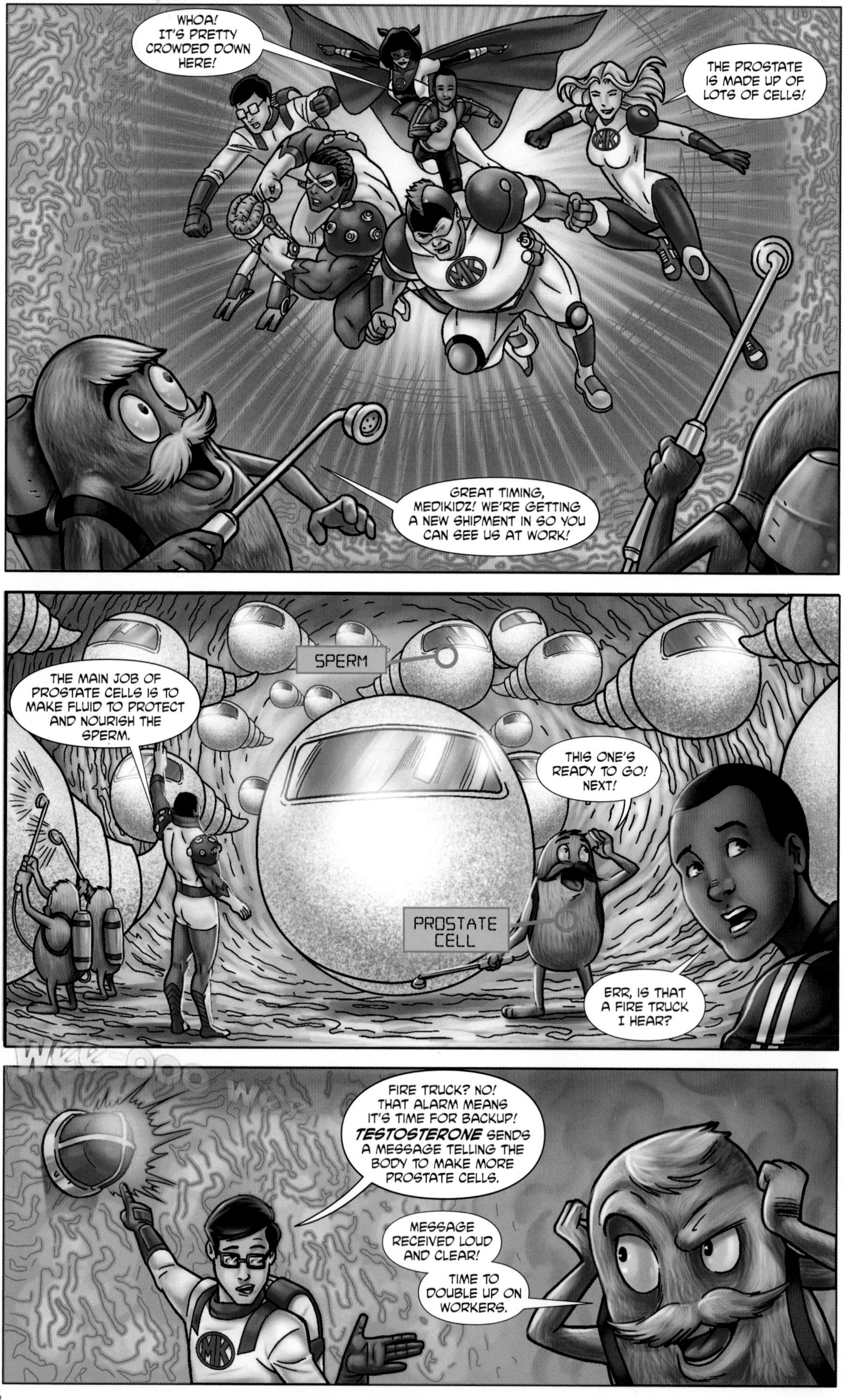
WHOA! IT'S PRETTY CROWDED DOWN HERE!
THE PROSTATE IS MADE UP OF LOTS OF CELLS!
GREAT TIMING, MEDIKIDZ! WE'RE GETTING A NEW SHIPMENT IN SO YOU CAN SEE US AT WORK!
SPERM
THE MAIN JOB OF PROSTATE CELLS IS TO MAKE FLUID TO PROTECT AND NOURISH THE SPERM.
THIS ONE'S READY TO GO! NEXT!
PROSTATE CELL
ERR, IS THAT A FIRE TRUCK I HEAR?
FIRE TRUCK? NO! THAT ALARM MEANS IT'S TIME FOR BACKUP! TESTOSTERONE SENDS A MESSAGE TELLING THE BODY TO MAKE MORE PROSTATE CELLS.
MESSAGE RECEIVED LOUD AND CLEAR!
TIME TO DOUBLE UP ON WORKERS.

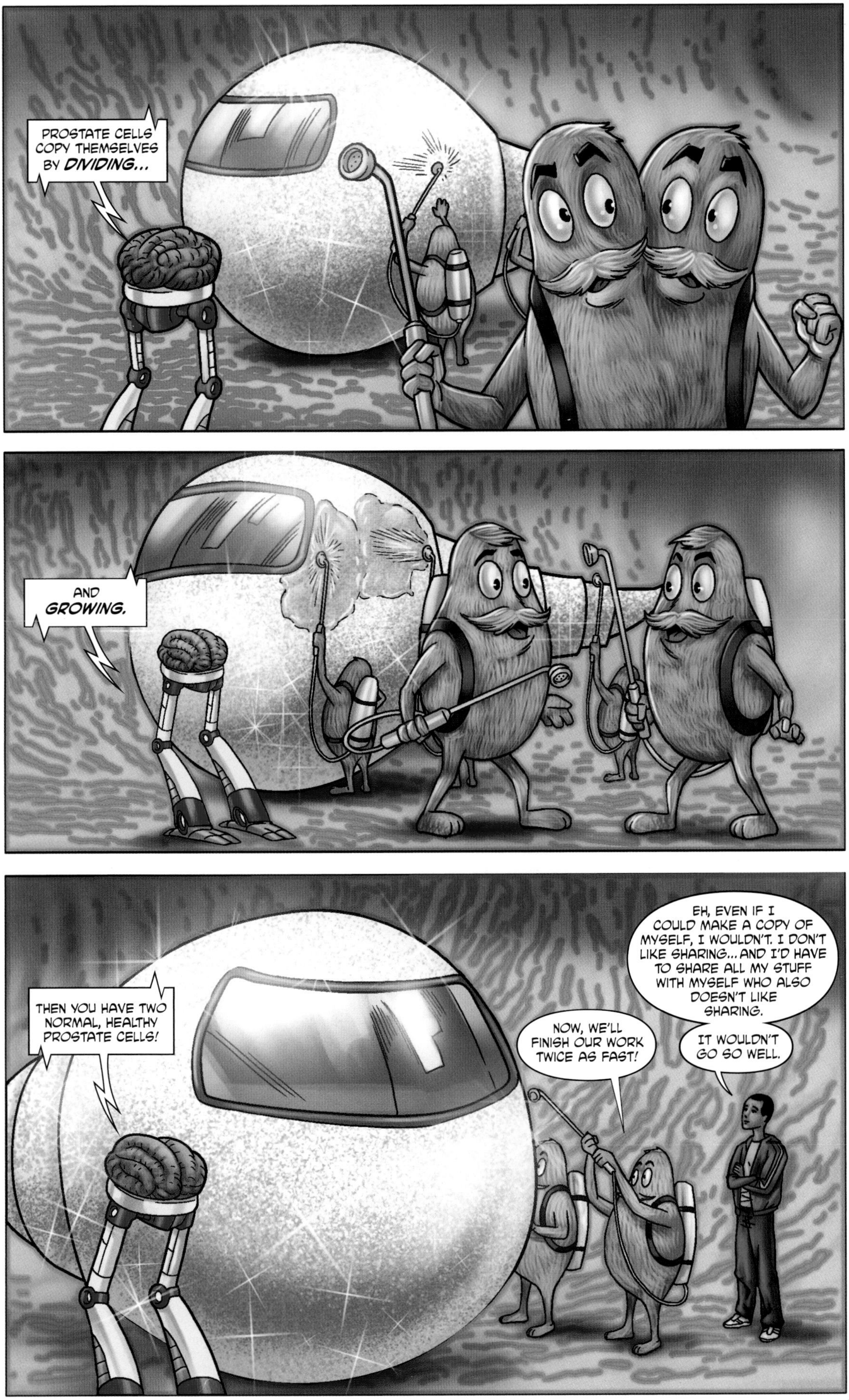
PROSTATE CELLS COPY THEMSELVES BY DIVIDING...
AND GROWING.
THEN YOU HAVE TWO NORMAL, HEALTHY PROSTATE CELLS!
NOW, WE'LL FINISH OUR WORK TWICE AS FAST!
EH, EVEN IF I COULD MAKE A COPY OF MYSELF, I WOULDN'T. I DON'T LIKE SHARING... AND I'D HAVE TO SHARE ALL MY STUFF WITH MYSELF WHO ALSO DOESN'T LIKE SHARING.
IT WOULDN'T GO SO WELL.

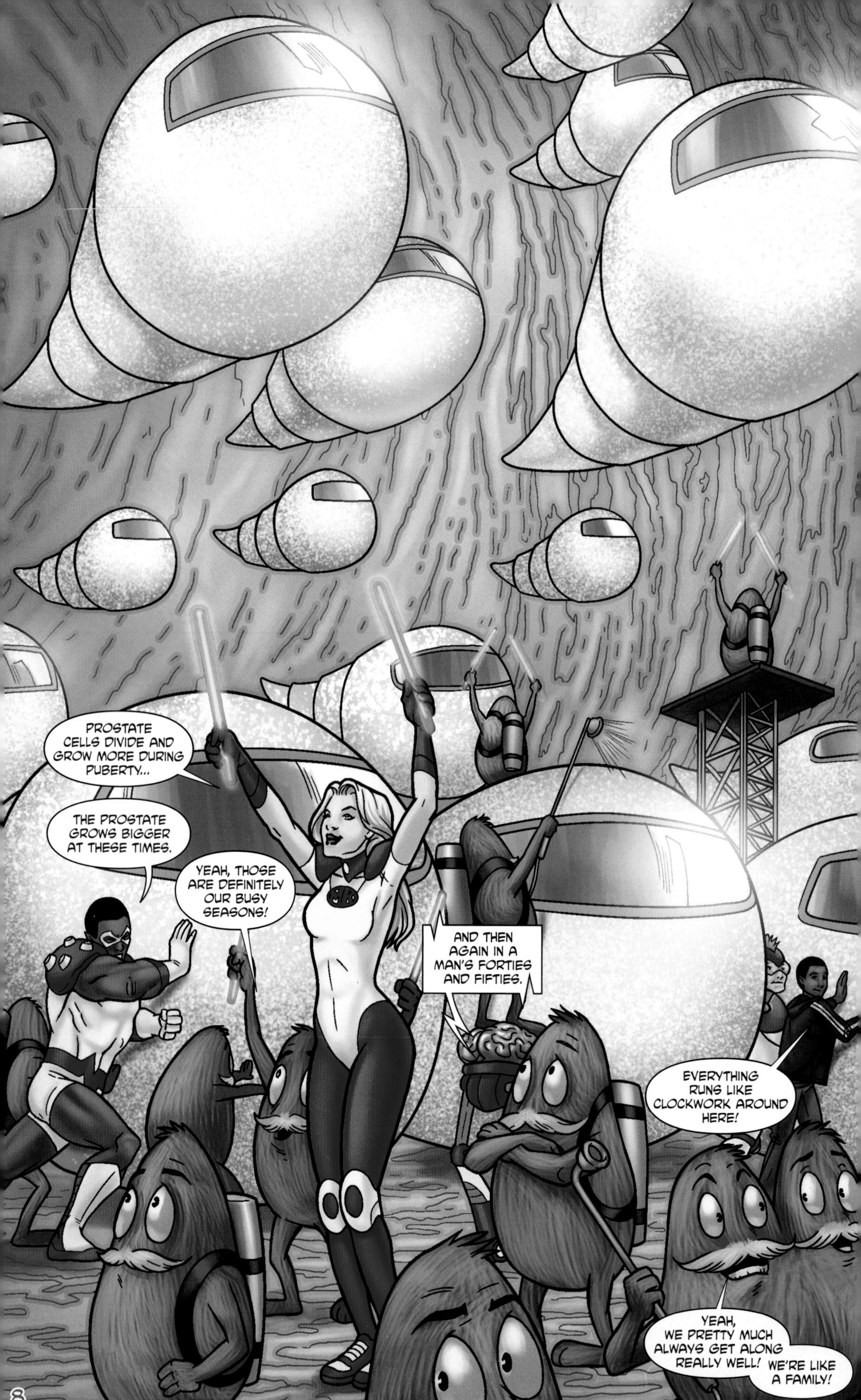
PROSTATE CELLS DIVIDE AND GROW MORE DURING PUBERTY...
THE PROSTATE GROWS BIGGER AT THESE TIMES.
YEAH, THOSE ARE DEFINITELY OUR BUSY SEASONS!
AND THEN AGAIN IN A MAN'S FORTIES AND FIFTIES.
EVERYTHING RUNS LIKE CLOCKWORK AROUND HERE!
YEAH, WE PRETTY MUCH ALWAYS GET ALONG REALLY WELL!
WE'RE LIKE A FAMILY!

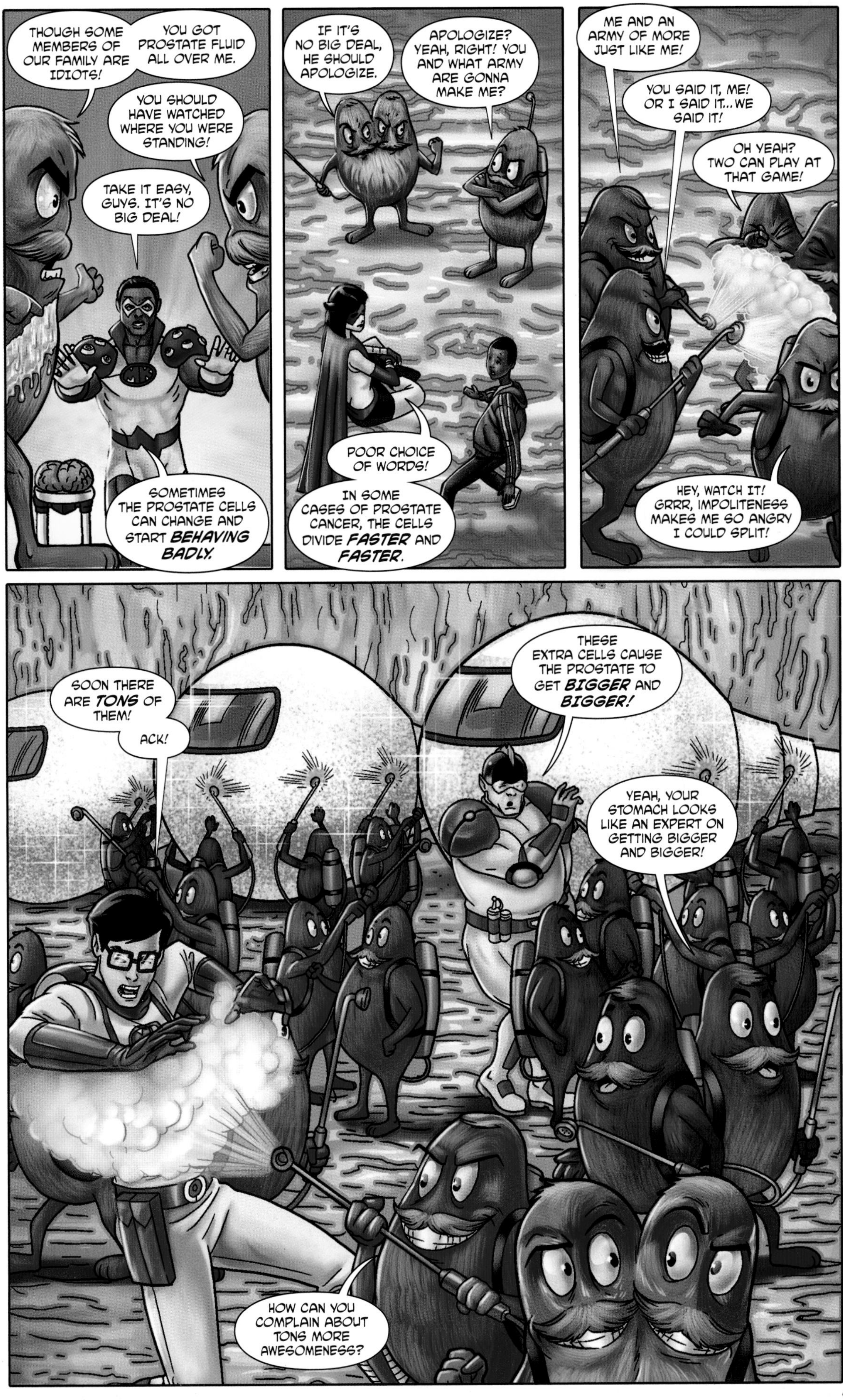
THOUGH SOME MEMBERS OF OUR FAMILY ARE IDIOTS!
YOU GOT PROSTATE FLUID ALL OVER ME.
YOU SHOULD HAVE WATCHED WHERE YOU WERE STANDING!
TAKE IT EASY, GUYS. IT'S NO BIG DEAL!
SOMETIMES THE PROSTATE CELLS CAN CHANGE AND START BEHAVING BADLY.
IF IT'S NO BIG DEAL, HE SHOULD APOLOGIZE.
APOLOGIZE? YEAH, RIGHT! YOU AND WHAT ARMY ARE GONNA MAKE ME?
POOR CHOICE OF WORDS!
IN SOME CASES OF PROSTATE CANCER, THE CELLS DIVIDE FASTER AND FASTER.
ME AND AN ARMY OF MORE JUST LIKE ME!
YOU SAID IT, ME! OR I SAID IT... WE SAID IT!
OH YEAH? TWO CAN PLAY AT THAT GAME!
HEY, WATCH IT! GRRR, IMPOLITENESS MAKES ME SO ANGRY I COULD SPLIT!
SOON THERE ARE TONS OF THEM!
ACK!
THESE EXTRA CELLS CAUSE THE PROSTATE TO GET BIGGER AND BIGGER!
YEAH, YOUR STOMACH LOOKS LIKE AN EXPERT ON GETTING BIGGER AND BIGGER!
HOW CAN YOU COMPLAIN ABOUT TONS MORE AWESOMENESS?

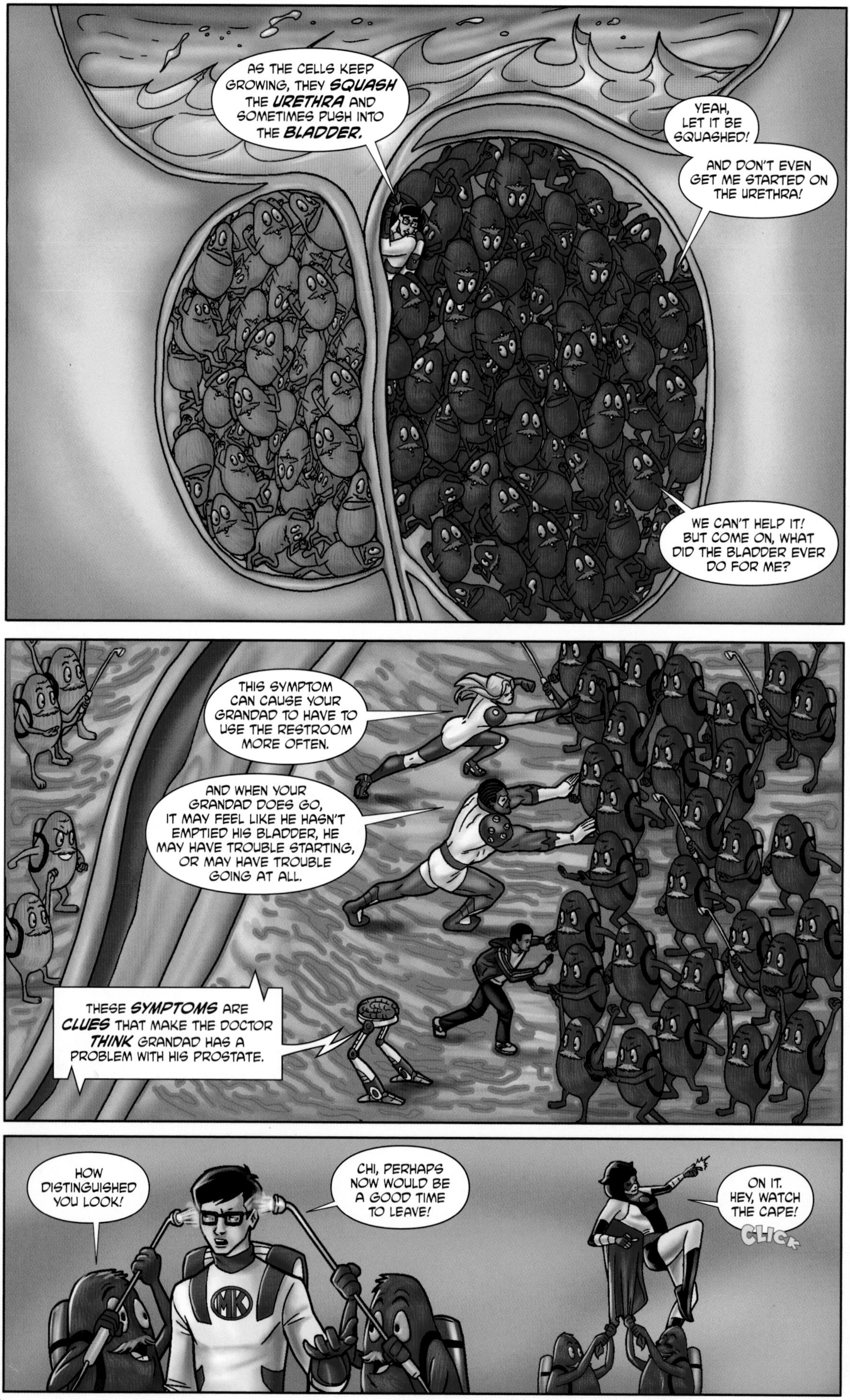
AS THE CELLS KEEP GROWING, THEY SQUASH THE URETHRA AND SOMETIMES PUSH INTO THE BLADDER.
YEAH, LET IT BE SQUASHED!
AND DON'T EVEN GET ME STARTED ON THE URETHRA!
WE CAN'T HELP IT! BUT COME ON, WHAT DID THE BLADDER EVER DO FOR ME?
THIS SYMPTOM CAN CAUSE YOUR GRANDAD TO HAVE TO USE THE RESTROOM MORE OFTEN.
AND WHEN YOUR GRANDAD DOES GO, IT MAY FEEL LIKE HE HASN'T EMPTIED HIS BLADDER, HE MAY HAVE TROUBLE STARTING, OR MAY HAVE TROUBLE GOING AT ALL.
THESE SYMPTOMS ARE CLUES THAT MAKE THE DOCTOR THINK GRANDAD HAS A PROBLEM WITH HIS PROSTATE.
HOW DISTINGUISHED YOU LOOK!
CHI, PERHAPS NOW WOULD BE A GOOD TIME TO LEAVE!
ON IT. HEY, WATCH THE CAPE!
CLICK

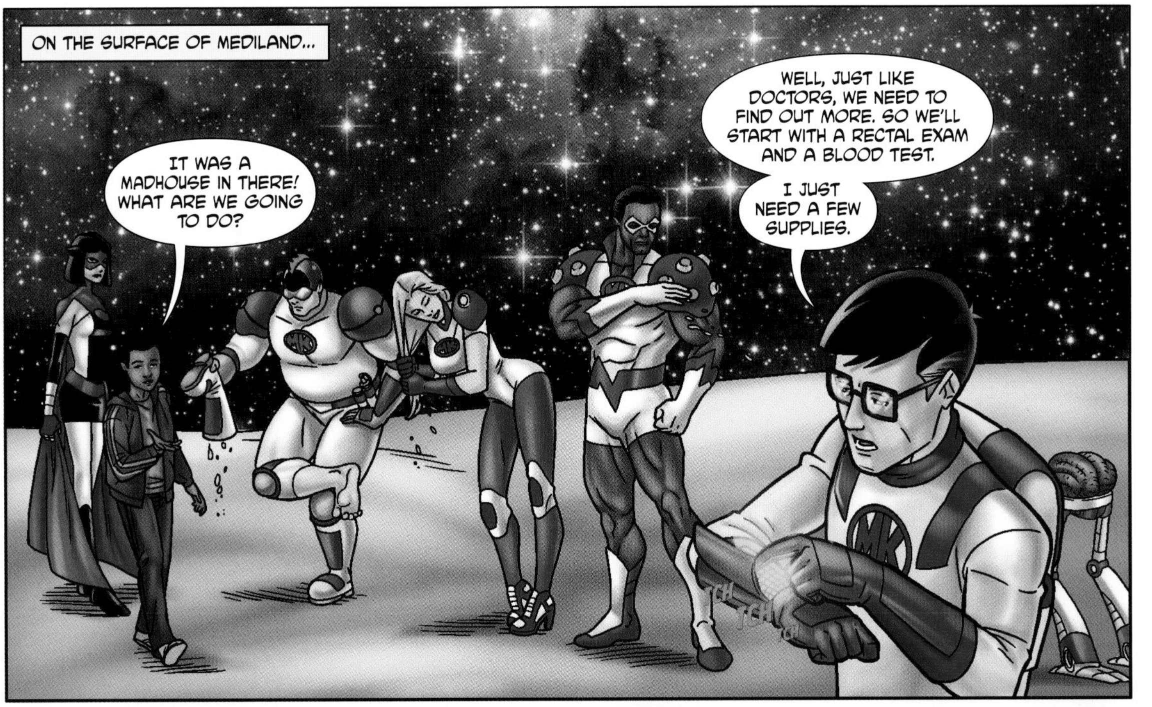
ON THE SURFACE OF MEDILAND...
IT WAS A MADHOUSE IN THERE! WHAT ARE WE GOING TO DO?
WELL, JUST LIKE DOCTORS, WE NEED TO FIND OUT MORE. SO WE'LL START WITH A RECTAL EXAM AND A BLOOD TEST.
I JUST NEED A FEW SUPPLIES.

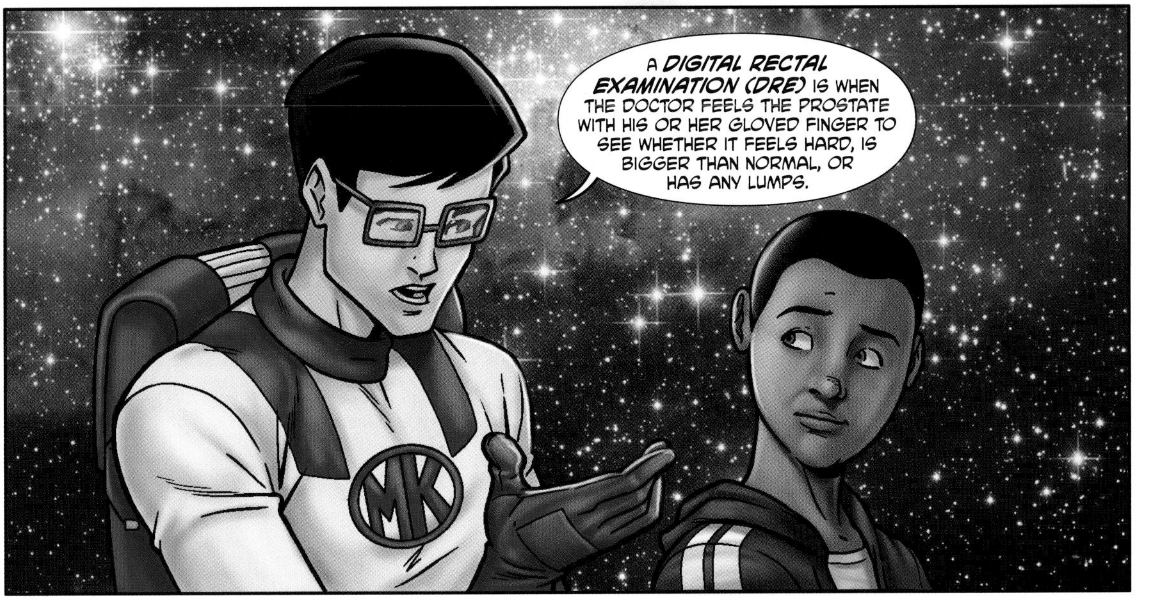
A ***DIGITAL RECTAL EXAMINATION (DRE)*** IS WHEN THE DOCTOR FEELS THE PROSTATE WITH HIS OR HER GLOVED FINGER TO SEE WHETHER IT FEELS HARD, IS BIGGER THAN NORMAL, OR HAS ANY LUMPS.

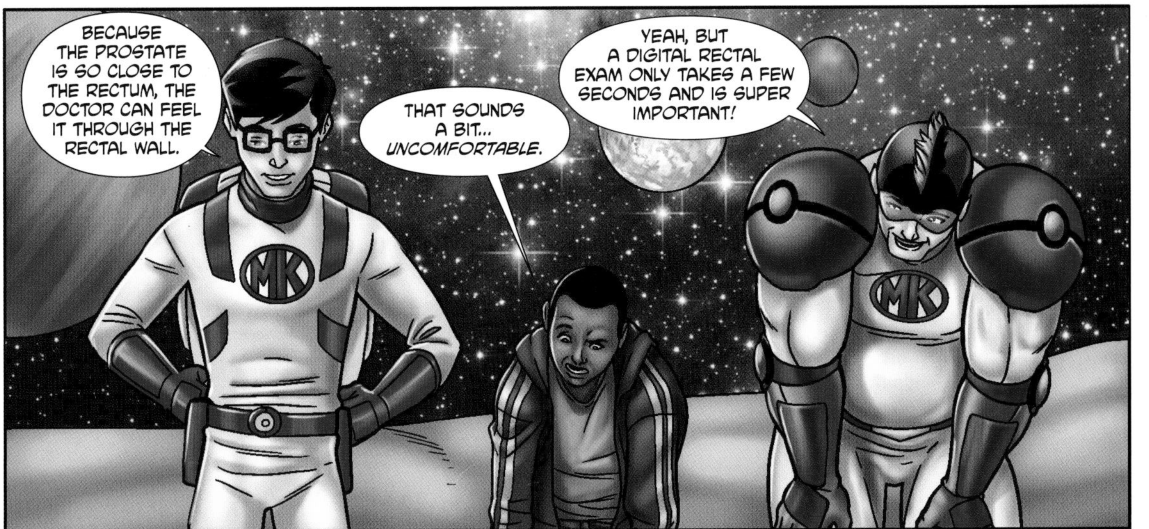
BECAUSE THE PROSTATE IS SO CLOSE TO THE RECTUM, THE DOCTOR CAN FEEL IT THROUGH THE RECTAL WALL.
THAT SOUNDS A BIT... *UNCOMFORTABLE.*
YEAH, BUT A DIGITAL RECTAL EXAM ONLY TAKES A FEW SECONDS AND IS SUPER IMPORTANT!

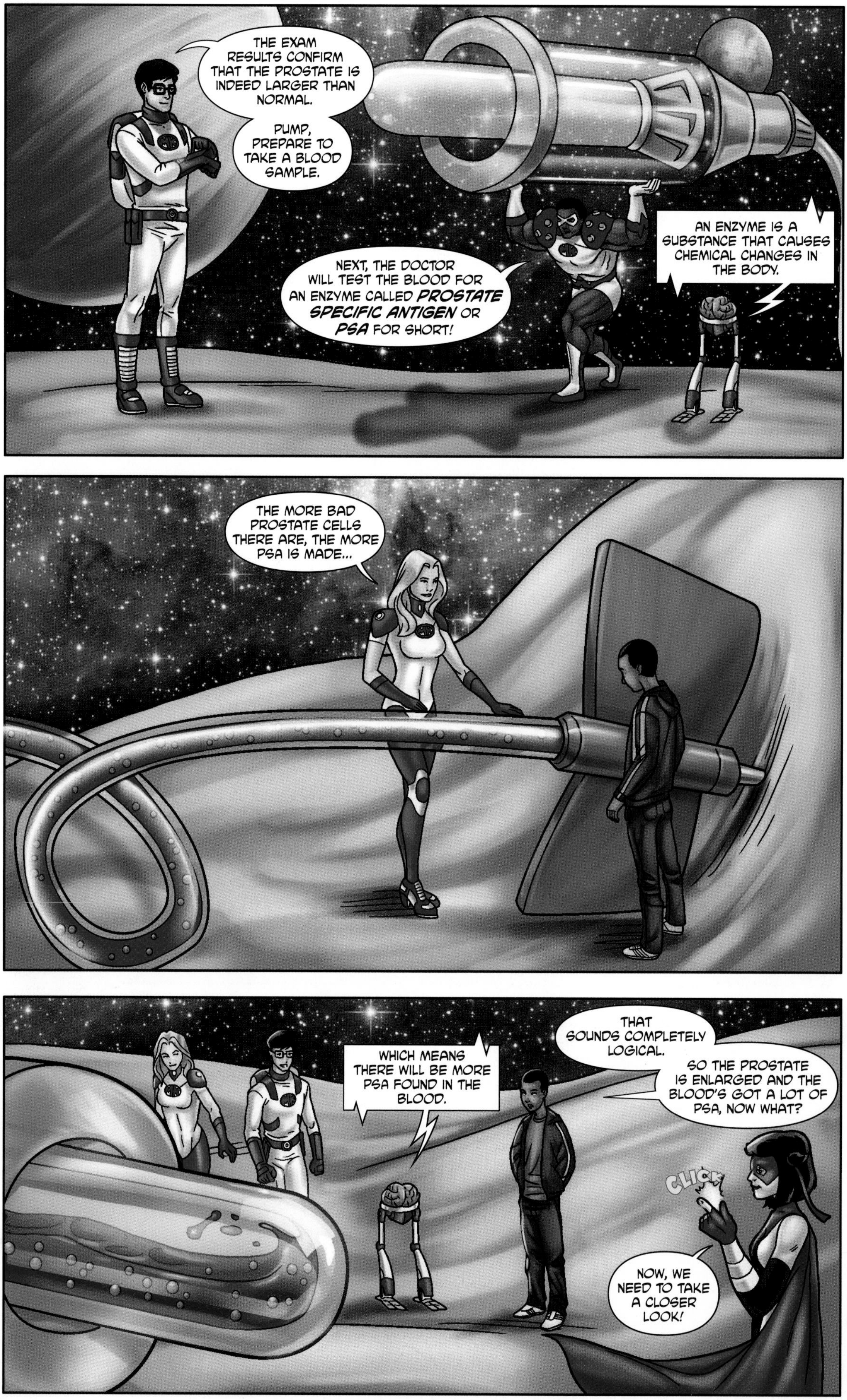
THE EXAM RESULTS CONFIRM THAT THE PROSTATE IS INDEED LARGER THAN NORMAL.
PUMP, PREPARE TO TAKE A BLOOD SAMPLE.
NEXT, THE DOCTOR WILL TEST THE BLOOD FOR AN ENZYME CALLED ***PROSTATE SPECIFIC ANTIGEN*** OR ***PSA*** FOR SHORT!
AN ENZYME IS A SUBSTANCE THAT CAUSES CHEMICAL CHANGES IN THE BODY.
THE MORE BAD PROSTATE CELLS THERE ARE, THE MORE PSA IS MADE...
WHICH MEANS THERE WILL BE MORE PSA FOUND IN THE BLOOD.
THAT SOUNDS COMPLETELY LOGICAL.
SO THE PROSTATE IS ENLARGED AND THE BLOOD'S GOT A LOT OF PSA, NOW WHAT?
CLICK
NOW, WE NEED TO TAKE A CLOSER LOOK!

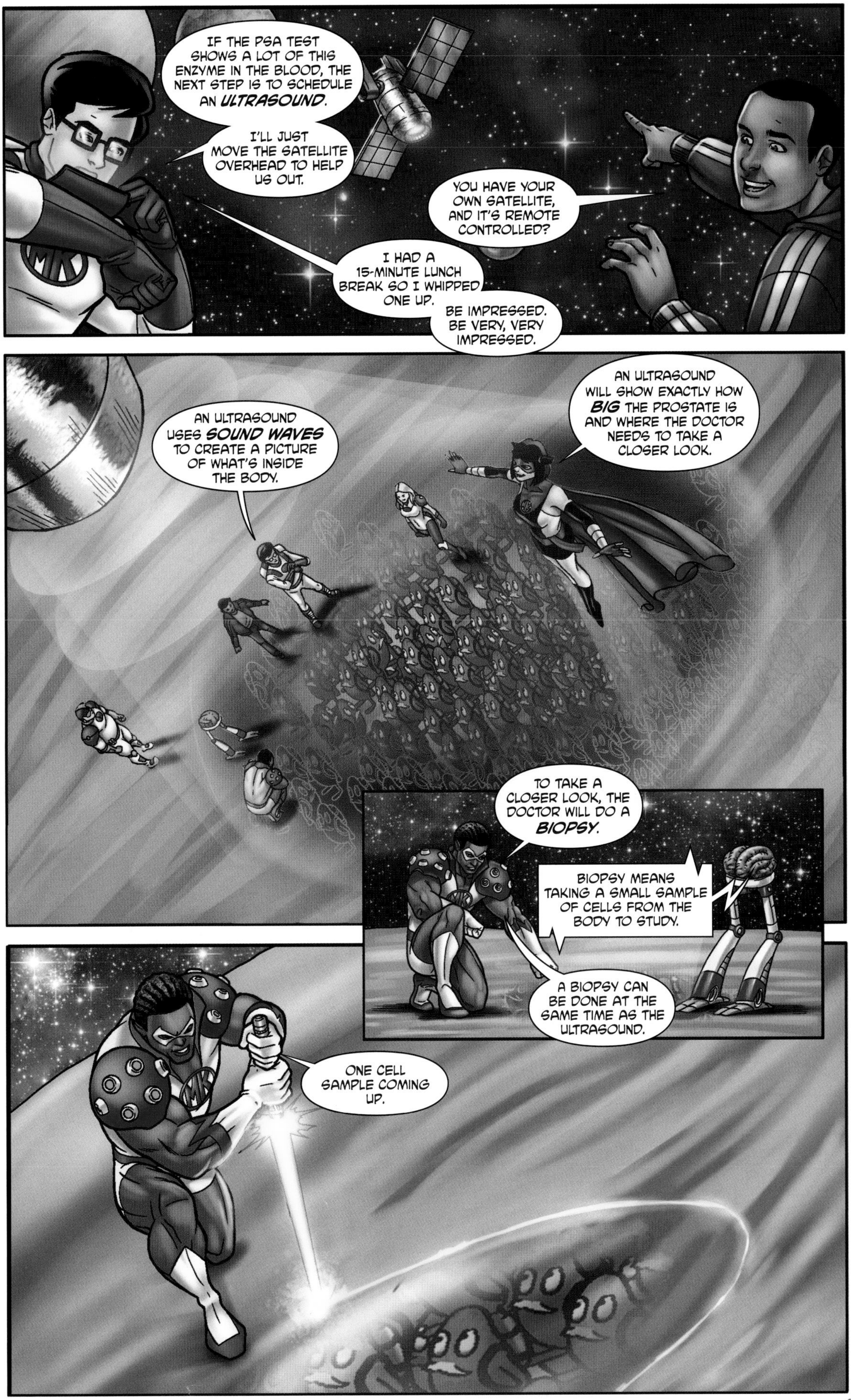

IF THE PSA TEST SHOWS A LOT OF THIS ENZYME IN THE BLOOD, THE NEXT STEP IS TO SCHEDULE AN ULTRASOUND.
I'LL JUST MOVE THE SATELLITE OVERHEAD TO HELP US OUT.
YOU HAVE YOUR OWN SATELLITE, AND IT'S REMOTE CONTROLLED?
I HAD A 15-MINUTE LUNCH BREAK SO I WHIPPED ONE UP.
BE IMPRESSED. BE VERY, VERY IMPRESSED.
AN ULTRASOUND USES SOUND WAVES TO CREATE A PICTURE OF WHAT'S INSIDE THE BODY.
AN ULTRASOUND WILL SHOW EXACTLY HOW BIG THE PROSTATE IS AND WHERE THE DOCTOR NEEDS TO TAKE A CLOSER LOOK.
TO TAKE A CLOSER LOOK, THE DOCTOR WILL DO A BIOPSY.
BIOPSY MEANS TAKING A SMALL SAMPLE OF CELLS FROM THE BODY TO STUDY.
A BIOPSY CAN BE DONE AT THE SAME TIME AS THE ULTRASOUND.
ONE CELL SAMPLE COMING UP.

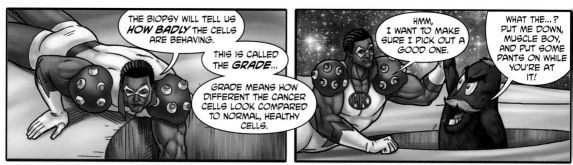

THE BIOPSY WILL TELL US *HOW BADLY* THE CELLS ARE BEHAVING.

THIS IS CALLED THE *GRADE*...

GRADE MEANS HOW DIFFERENT THE CANCER CELLS LOOK COMPARED TO NORMAL, HEALTHY CELLS.

HMM, I WANT TO MAKE SURE I PICK OUT A GOOD ONE.

WHAT THE...? PUT ME DOWN, MUSCLE BOY, AND PUT SOME PANTS ON WHILE YOU'RE AT IT!

HE'LL DO JUST FINE.

THE BIOPSY WILL TELL US WHETHER THE CELLS ARE *BENIGN* OR *MALIGNANT*.

HEY, PERSONAL SPACE, BUDDY!

BENIGN LUMPS ARE MADE UP OF CELLS THAT KEEP TO THEMSELVES AND DON'T DISRUPT THE CELLS AROUND THEM.

THESE CELLS ARE *NOT CANCER.*

THIS CONDITION IS COMMON IN MEN OVER 50 BECAUSE THIS AGE IS GENERALLY WHEN THE PROSTATE STARTS GROWING AGAIN.

IT'S CALLED *BENIGN PROSTATIC HYPERPLASIA.*

PLEASE, SIR, I JUST WANT TO GO BACK TO PLAYING WITH MY BROTHERS. I PROMISE TO BE GOOD.

HMM, YOU DO SEEM TOO ADORABLE TO BE DANGEROUS.

WELL, YOU KNOW WHAT THEY SAY...

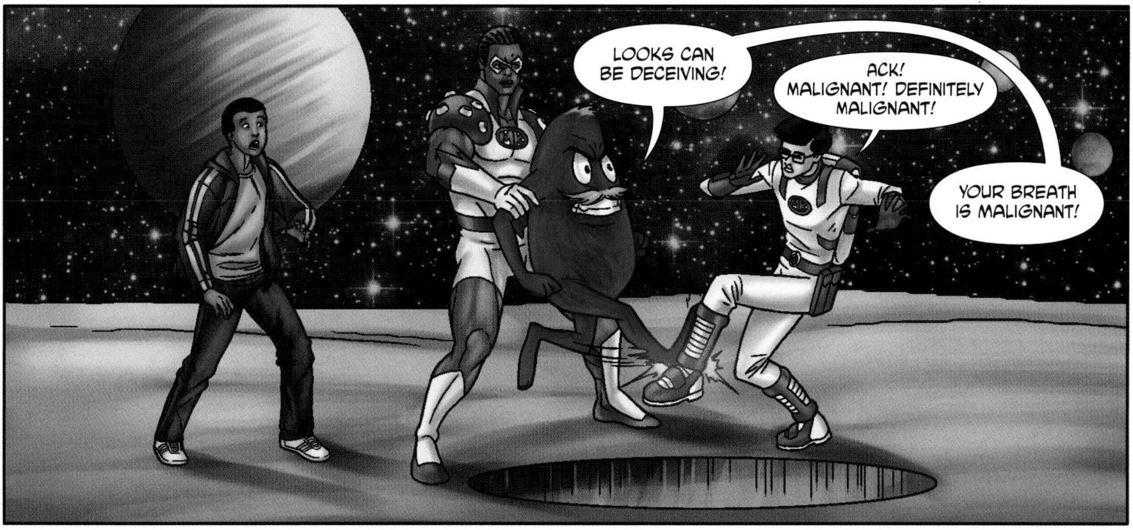
LOOKS CAN BE DECEIVING!
ACK! MALIGNANT! DEFINITELY MALIGNANT!
YOUR BREATH IS MALIGNANT!

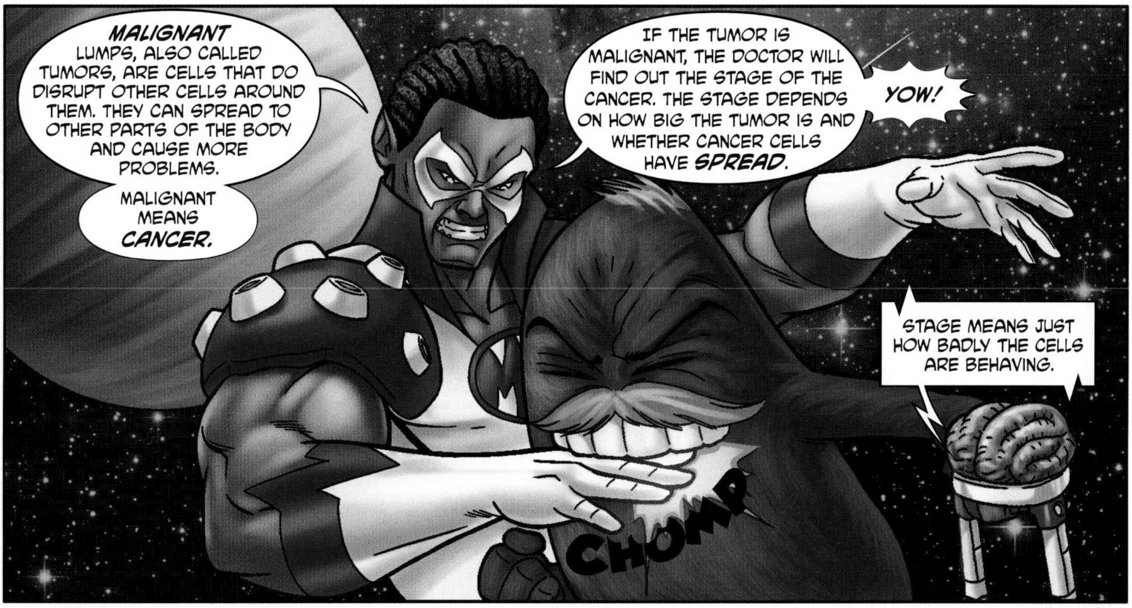
MALIGNANT LUMPS, ALSO CALLED TUMORS, ARE CELLS THAT DO DISRUPT OTHER CELLS AROUND THEM. THEY CAN SPREAD TO OTHER PARTS OF THE BODY AND CAUSE MORE PROBLEMS.
MALIGNANT MEANS CANCER.
IF THE TUMOR IS MALIGNANT, THE DOCTOR WILL FIND OUT THE STAGE OF THE CANCER. THE STAGE DEPENDS ON HOW BIG THE TUMOR IS AND WHETHER CANCER CELLS HAVE SPREAD.
YOW!
STAGE MEANS JUST HOW BADLY THE CELLS ARE BEHAVING.
CHOMP

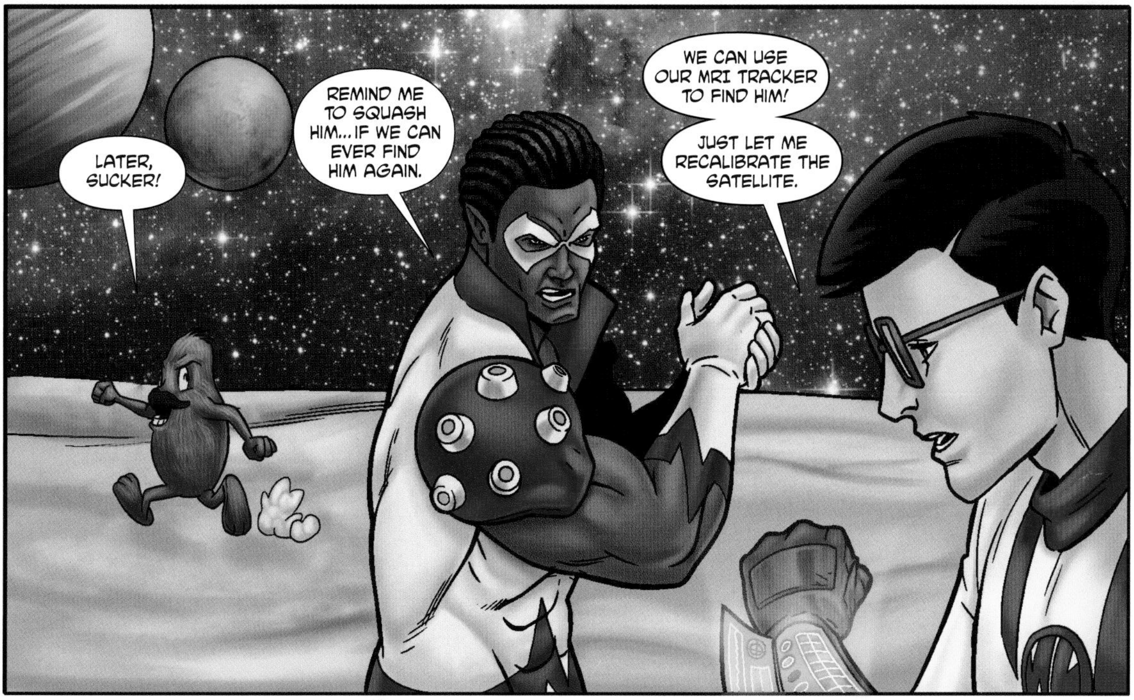
LATER, SUCKER!
REMIND ME TO SQUASH HIM...IF WE CAN EVER FIND HIM AGAIN.
WE CAN USE OUR MRI TRACKER TO FIND HIM!
JUST LET ME RECALIBRATE THE SATELLITE.

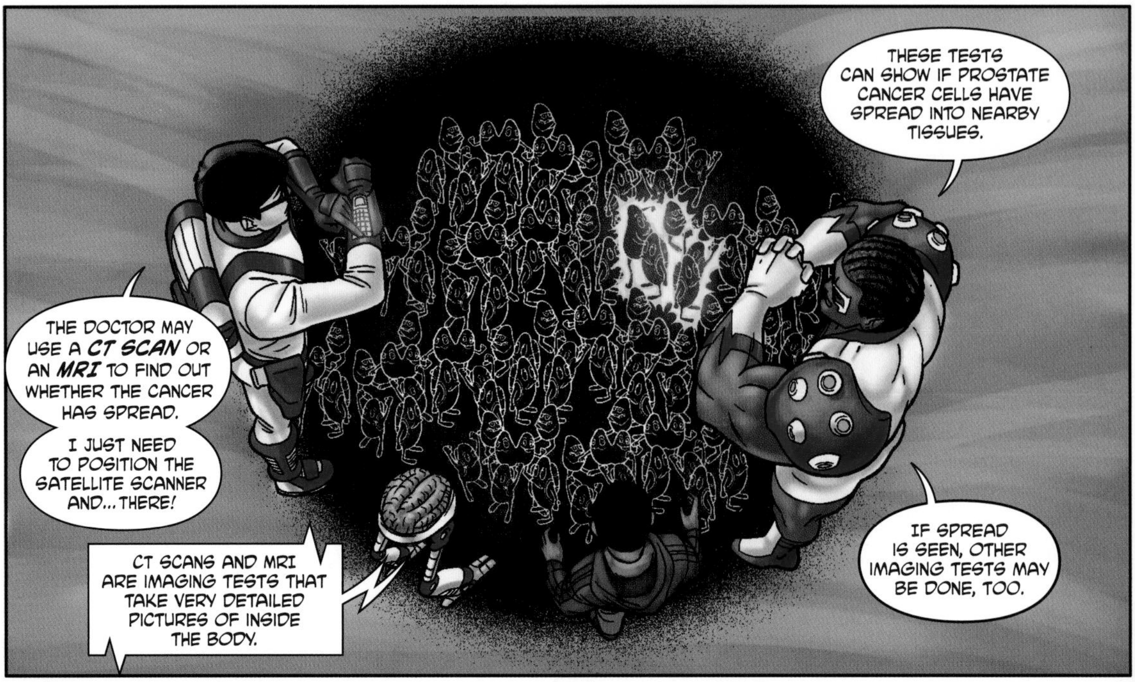
THESE TESTS CAN SHOW IF PROSTATE CANCER CELLS HAVE SPREAD INTO NEARBY TISSUES.
THE DOCTOR MAY USE A *CT SCAN* OR AN *MRI* TO FIND OUT WHETHER THE CANCER HAS SPREAD.
I JUST NEED TO POSITION THE SATELLITE SCANNER AND... THERE!
CT SCANS AND MRI ARE IMAGING TESTS THAT TAKE VERY DETAILED PICTURES OF INSIDE THE BODY.
IF SPREAD IS SEEN, OTHER IMAGING TESTS MAY BE DONE, TOO.

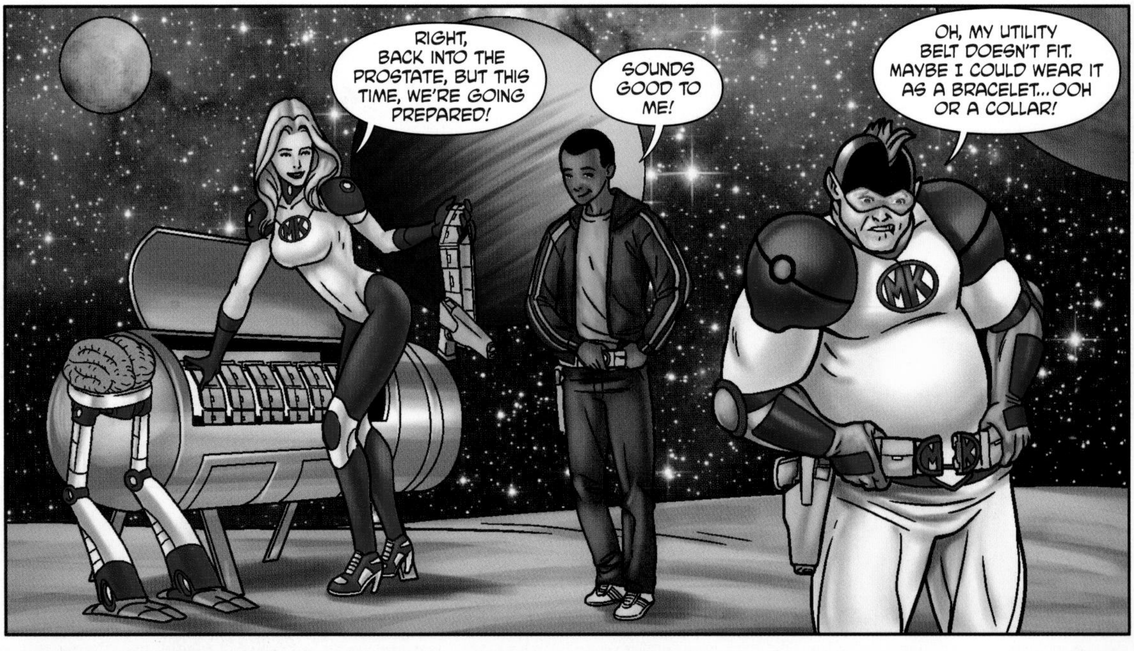
RIGHT, BACK INTO THE PROSTATE, BUT THIS TIME, WE'RE GOING PREPARED!
SOUNDS GOOD TO ME!
OH, MY UTILITY BELT DOESN'T FIT. MAYBE I COULD WEAR IT AS A BRACELET... OOH OR A COLLAR!

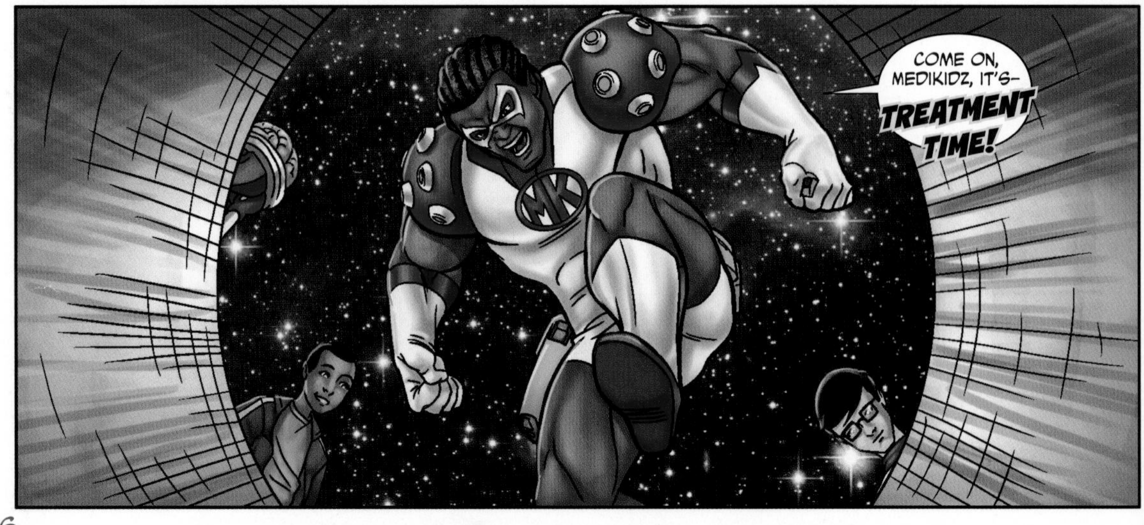
COME ON, MEDIKIDZ, IT'S–
TREATMENT TIME!

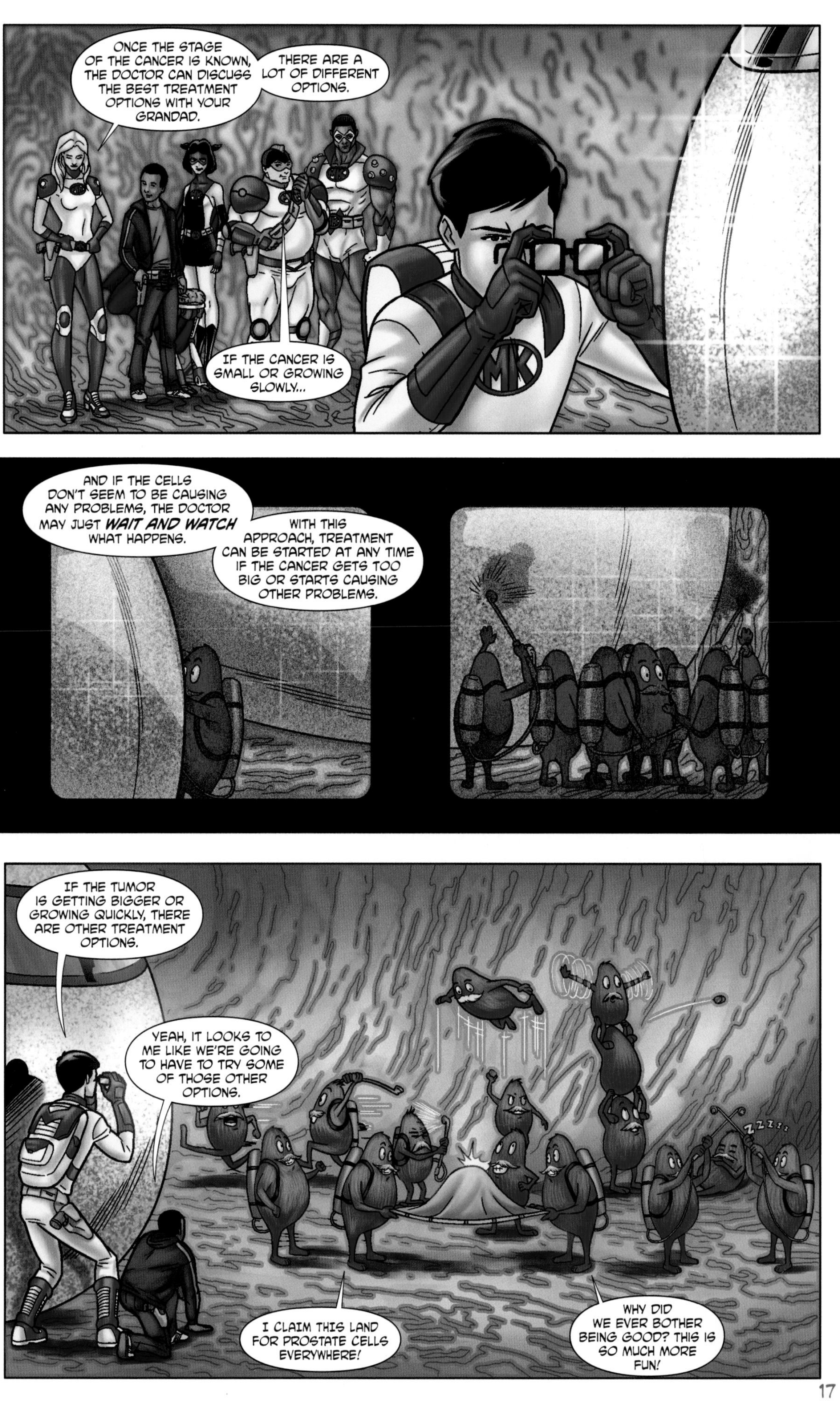

ONCE THE STAGE OF THE CANCER IS KNOWN, THE DOCTOR CAN DISCUSS THE BEST TREATMENT OPTIONS WITH YOUR GRANDAD.
THERE ARE A LOT OF DIFFERENT OPTIONS.
IF THE CANCER IS SMALL OR GROWING SLOWLY...
AND IF THE CELLS DON'T SEEM TO BE CAUSING ANY PROBLEMS, THE DOCTOR MAY JUST WAIT AND WATCH WHAT HAPPENS.
WITH THIS APPROACH, TREATMENT CAN BE STARTED AT ANY TIME IF THE CANCER GETS TOO BIG OR STARTS CAUSING OTHER PROBLEMS.
IF THE TUMOR IS GETTING BIGGER OR GROWING QUICKLY, THERE ARE OTHER TREATMENT OPTIONS.
YEAH, IT LOOKS TO ME LIKE WE'RE GOING TO HAVE TO TRY SOME OF THOSE OTHER OPTIONS.
ZZZZZ
I CLAIM THIS LAND FOR PROSTATE CELLS EVERYWHERE!
WHY DID WE EVER BOTHER BEING GOOD? THIS IS SO MUCH MORE FUN!

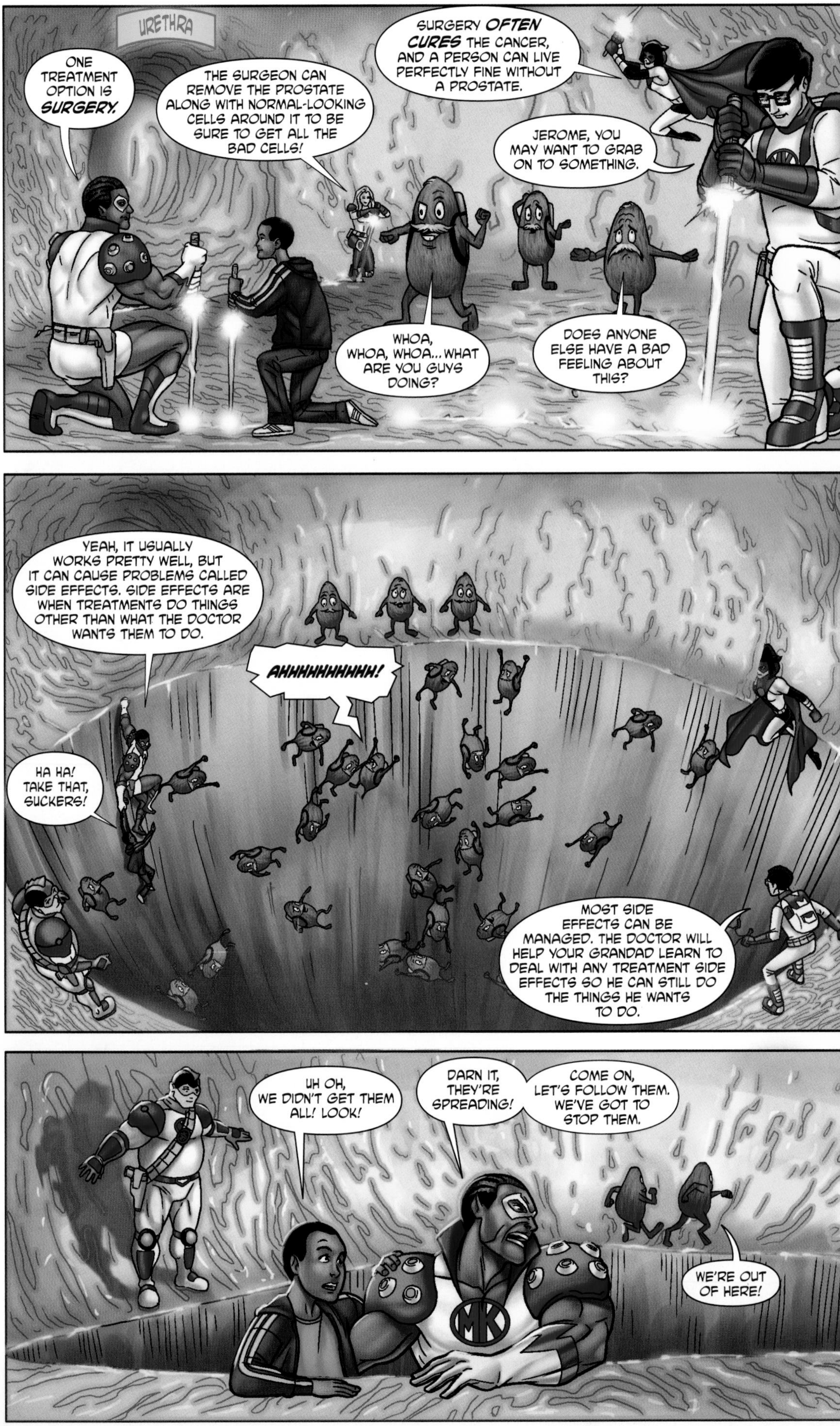
URETHRA
ONE TREATMENT OPTION IS **SURGERY.**
THE SURGEON CAN REMOVE THE PROSTATE ALONG WITH NORMAL-LOOKING CELLS AROUND IT TO BE SURE TO GET ALL THE BAD CELLS!
SURGERY **OFTEN CURES** THE CANCER, AND A PERSON CAN LIVE PERFECTLY FINE WITHOUT A PROSTATE.
JEROME, YOU MAY WANT TO GRAB ON TO SOMETHING.
WHOA, WHOA, WHOA... WHAT ARE YOU GUYS DOING?
DOES ANYONE ELSE HAVE A BAD FEELING ABOUT THIS?
YEAH, IT USUALLY WORKS PRETTY WELL, BUT IT CAN CAUSE PROBLEMS CALLED SIDE EFFECTS. SIDE EFFECTS ARE WHEN TREATMENTS DO THINGS OTHER THAN WHAT THE DOCTOR WANTS THEM TO DO.
AHHHHHHHHHH!
HA HA! TAKE THAT, SUCKERS!
MOST SIDE EFFECTS CAN BE MANAGED. THE DOCTOR WILL HELP YOUR GRANDAD LEARN TO DEAL WITH ANY TREATMENT SIDE EFFECTS SO HE CAN STILL DO THE THINGS HE WANTS TO DO.
UH OH, WE DIDN'T GET THEM ALL! LOOK!
DARN IT, THEY'RE SPREADING!
COME ON, LET'S FOLLOW THEM. WE'VE GOT TO STOP THEM.
WE'RE OUT OF HERE!
MK

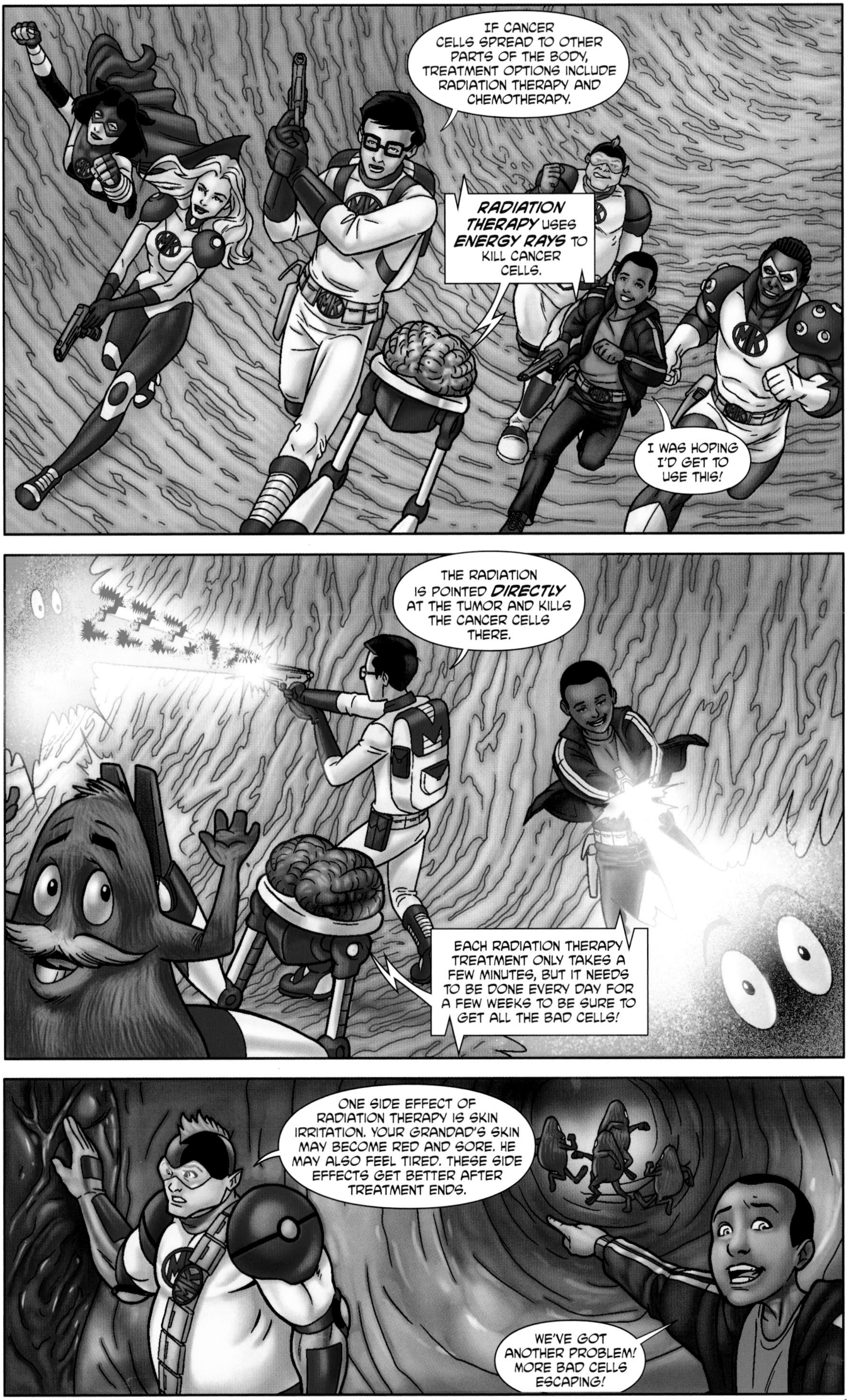
IF CANCER CELLS SPREAD TO OTHER PARTS OF THE BODY, TREATMENT OPTIONS INCLUDE RADIATION THERAPY AND CHEMOTHERAPY.
RADIATION THERAPY USES ENERGY RAYS TO KILL CANCER CELLS.
I WAS HOPING I'D GET TO USE THIS!
THE RADIATION IS POINTED DIRECTLY AT THE TUMOR AND KILLS THE CANCER CELLS THERE.
EACH RADIATION THERAPY TREATMENT ONLY TAKES A FEW MINUTES, BUT IT NEEDS TO BE DONE EVERY DAY FOR A FEW WEEKS TO BE SURE TO GET ALL THE BAD CELLS!
ONE SIDE EFFECT OF RADIATION THERAPY IS SKIN IRRITATION. YOUR GRANDAD'S SKIN MAY BECOME RED AND SORE. HE MAY ALSO FEEL TIRED. THESE SIDE EFFECTS GET BETTER AFTER TREATMENT ENDS.
WE'VE GOT ANOTHER PROBLEM! MORE BAD CELLS ESCAPING!

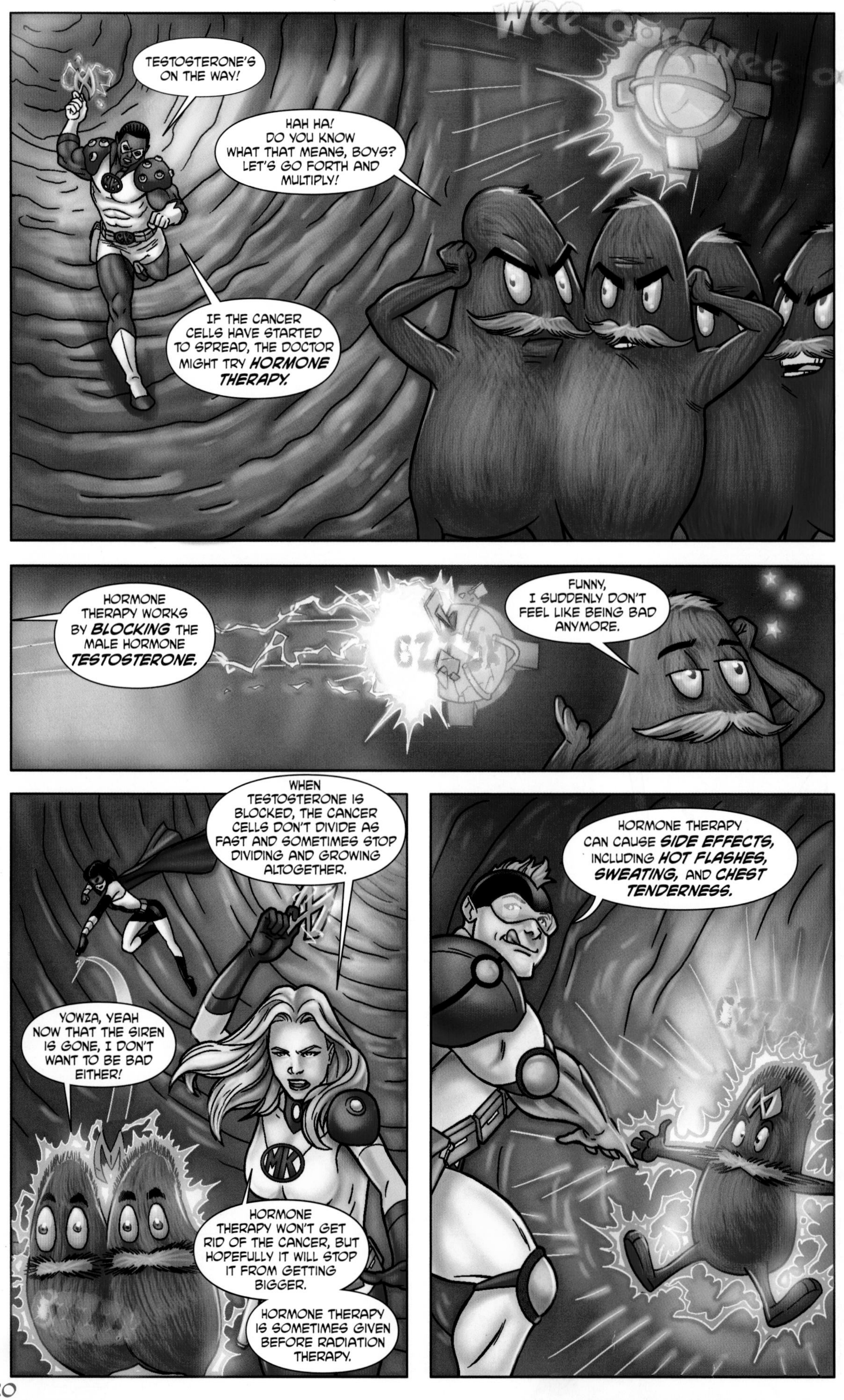
TESTOSTERONE'S ON THE WAY!
HAH HA! DO YOU KNOW WHAT THAT MEANS, BOYS? LET'S GO FORTH AND MULTIPLY!
IF THE CANCER CELLS HAVE STARTED TO SPREAD, THE DOCTOR MIGHT TRY *HORMONE THERAPY.*
HORMONE THERAPY WORKS BY *BLOCKING* THE MALE HORMONE *TESTOSTERONE.*
FUNNY, I SUDDENLY DON'T FEEL LIKE BEING BAD ANYMORE.
WHEN TESTOSTERONE IS BLOCKED, THE CANCER CELLS DON'T DIVIDE AS FAST AND SOMETIMES STOP DIVIDING AND GROWING ALTOGETHER.
YOWZA, YEAH NOW THAT THE SIREN IS GONE, I DON'T WANT TO BE BAD EITHER!
HORMONE THERAPY WON'T GET RID OF THE CANCER, BUT HOPEFULLY IT WILL STOP IT FROM GETTING BIGGER.
HORMONE THERAPY IS SOMETIMES GIVEN BEFORE RADIATION THERAPY.
HORMONE THERAPY CAN CAUSE *SIDE EFFECTS,* INCLUDING *HOT FLASHES, SWEATING,* AND *CHEST TENDERNESS.*

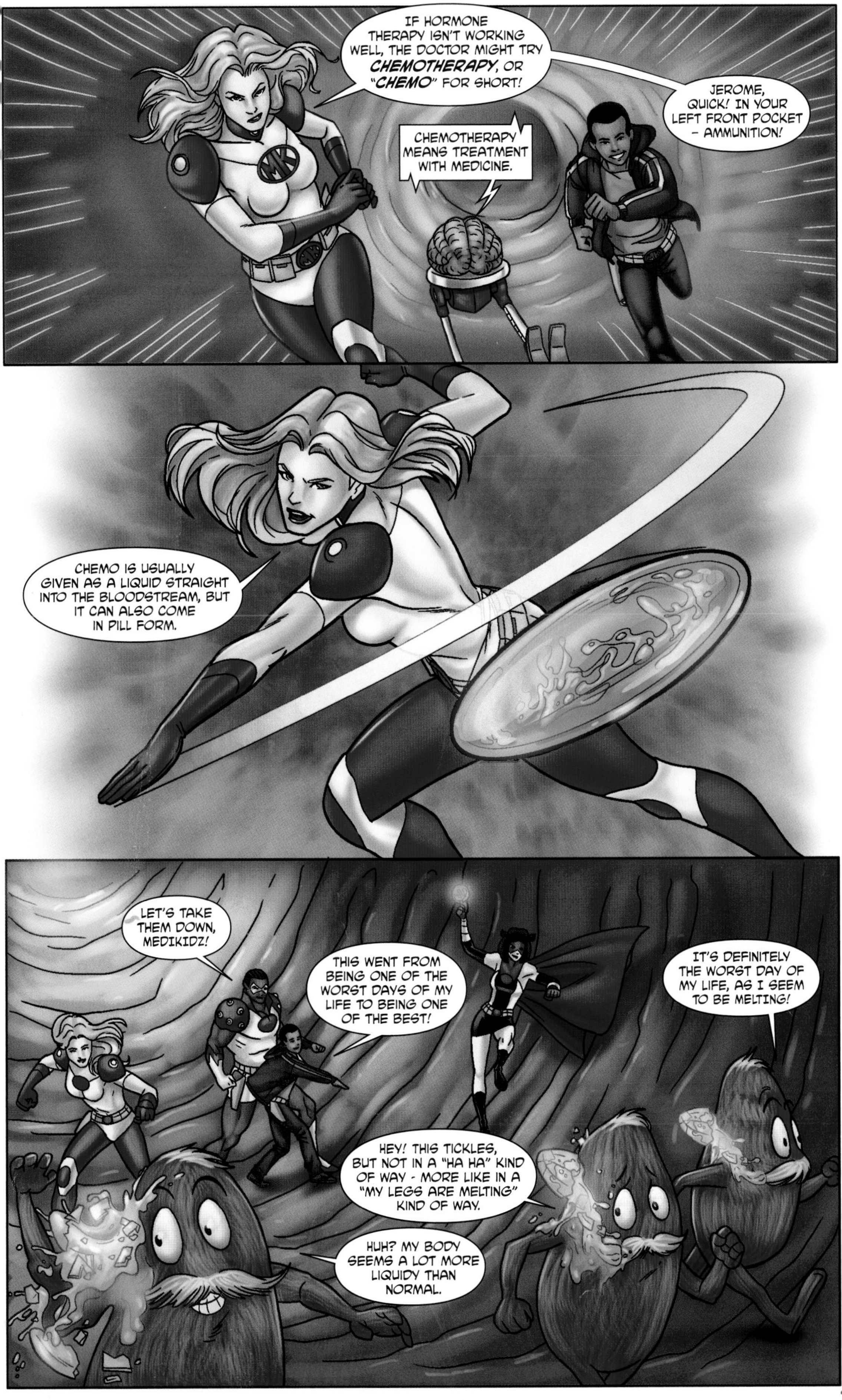
IF HORMONE THERAPY ISN'T WORKING WELL, THE DOCTOR MIGHT TRY CHEMOTHERAPY, OR "CHEMO" FOR SHORT!
JEROME, QUICK! IN YOUR LEFT FRONT POCKET – AMMUNITION!
CHEMOTHERAPY MEANS TREATMENT WITH MEDICINE.
CHEMO IS USUALLY GIVEN AS A LIQUID STRAIGHT INTO THE BLOODSTREAM, BUT IT CAN ALSO COME IN PILL FORM.
LET'S TAKE THEM DOWN, MEDIKIDZ!
THIS WENT FROM BEING ONE OF THE WORST DAYS OF MY LIFE TO BEING ONE OF THE BEST!
IT'S DEFINITELY THE WORST DAY OF MY LIFE, AS I SEEM TO BE MELTING!
HEY! THIS TICKLES, BUT NOT IN A "HA HA" KIND OF WAY - MORE LIKE IN A "MY LEGS ARE MELTING" KIND OF WAY.
HUH? MY BODY SEEMS A LOT MORE LIQUIDY THAN NORMAL.

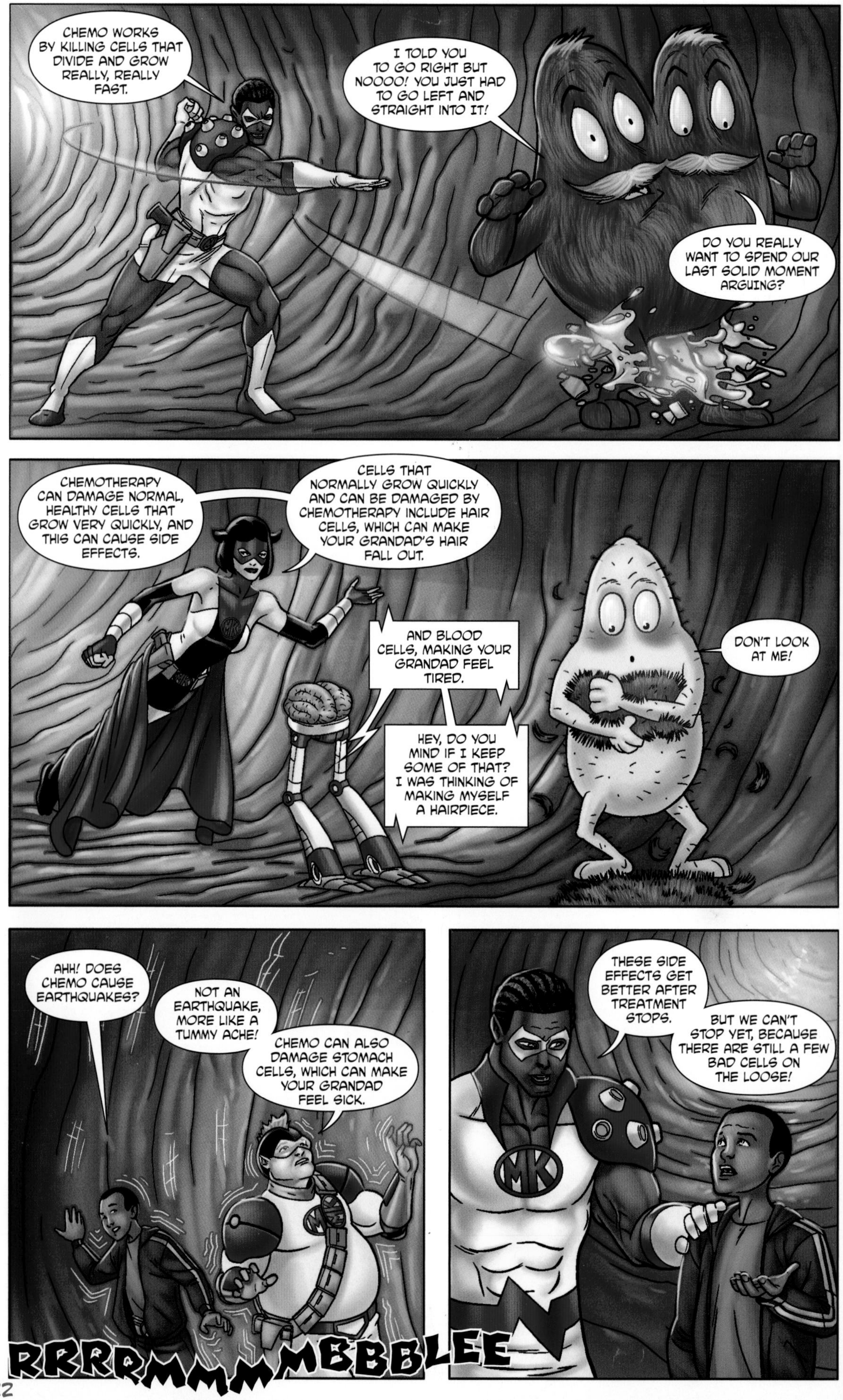
CHEMO WORKS BY KILLING CELLS THAT DIVIDE AND GROW REALLY, REALLY FAST.
I TOLD YOU TO GO RIGHT BUT NOOOO! YOU JUST HAD TO GO LEFT AND STRAIGHT INTO IT!
DO YOU REALLY WANT TO SPEND OUR LAST SOLID MOMENT ARGUING?
CHEMOTHERAPY CAN DAMAGE NORMAL, HEALTHY CELLS THAT GROW VERY QUICKLY, AND THIS CAN CAUSE SIDE EFFECTS.
CELLS THAT NORMALLY GROW QUICKLY AND CAN BE DAMAGED BY CHEMOTHERAPY INCLUDE HAIR CELLS, WHICH CAN MAKE YOUR GRANDAD'S HAIR FALL OUT.
AND BLOOD CELLS, MAKING YOUR GRANDAD FEEL TIRED.
DON'T LOOK AT ME!
HEY, DO YOU MIND IF I KEEP SOME OF THAT? I WAS THINKING OF MAKING MYSELF A HAIRPIECE.
AHH! DOES CHEMO CAUSE EARTHQUAKES?
NOT AN EARTHQUAKE, MORE LIKE A TUMMY ACHE!
CHEMO CAN ALSO DAMAGE STOMACH CELLS, WHICH CAN MAKE YOUR GRANDAD FEEL SICK.
RRRRMMMMEBBBLEE
THESE SIDE EFFECTS GET BETTER AFTER TREATMENT STOPS.
BUT WE CAN'T STOP YET, BECAUSE THERE ARE STILL A FEW BAD CELLS ON THE LOOSE!

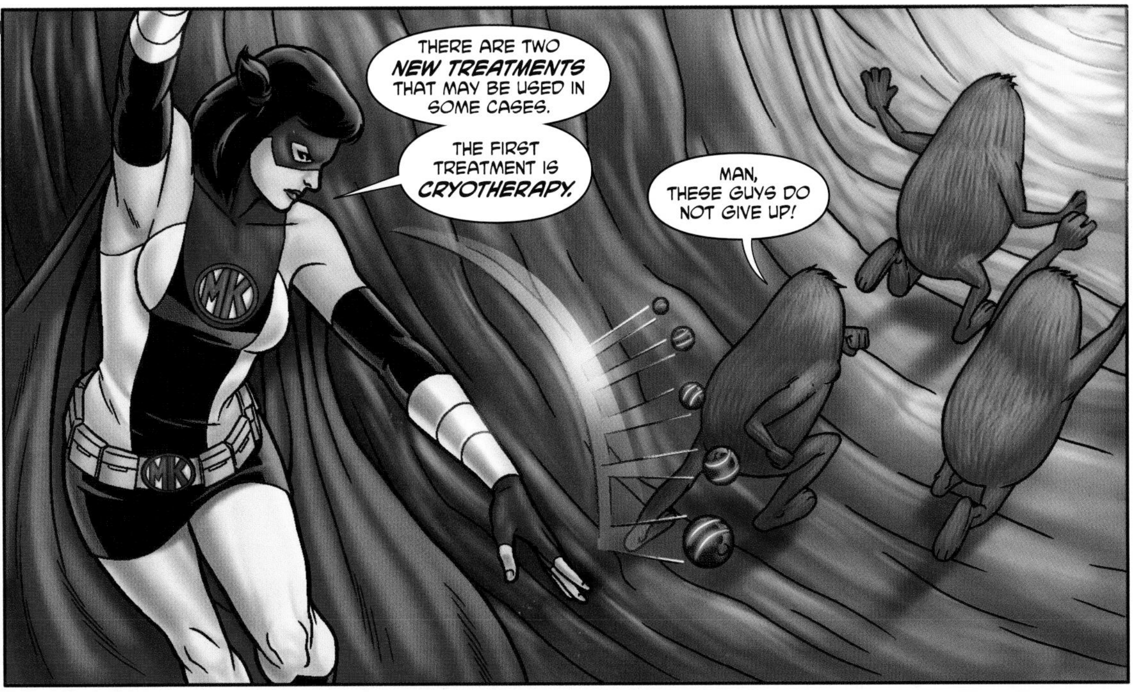
THERE ARE TWO NEW TREATMENTS THAT MAY BE USED IN SOME CASES.
THE FIRST TREATMENT IS CRYOTHERAPY.
MAN, THESE GUYS DO NOT GIVE UP!

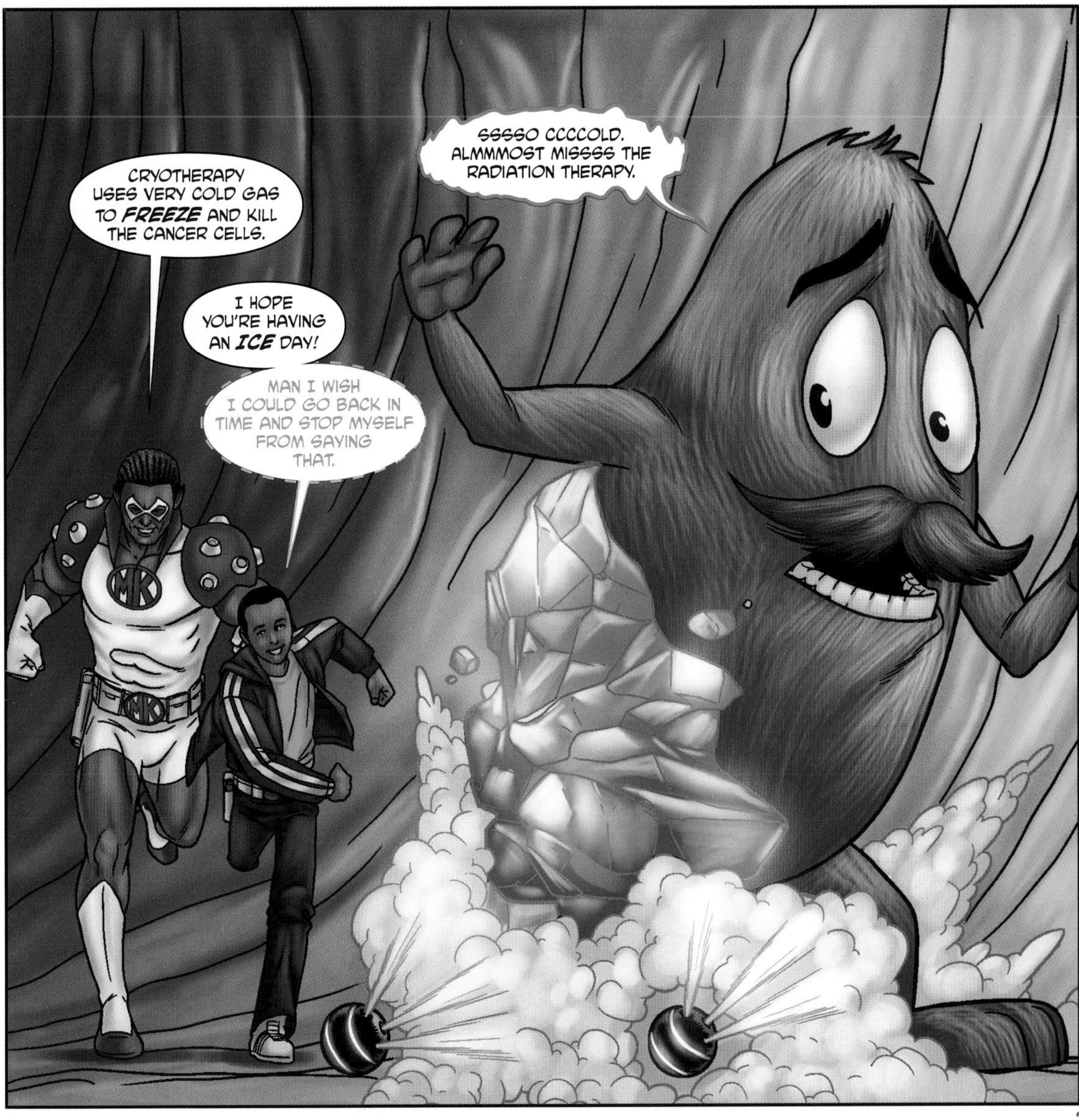
CRYOTHERAPY USES VERY COLD GAS TO FREEZE AND KILL THE CANCER CELLS.
I HOPE YOU'RE HAVING AN ICE DAY!
MAN I WISH I COULD GO BACK IN TIME AND STOP MYSELF FROM SAYING THAT.
SSSSO CCCCOLD. ALMMMOST MISSSS THE RADIATION THERAPY.

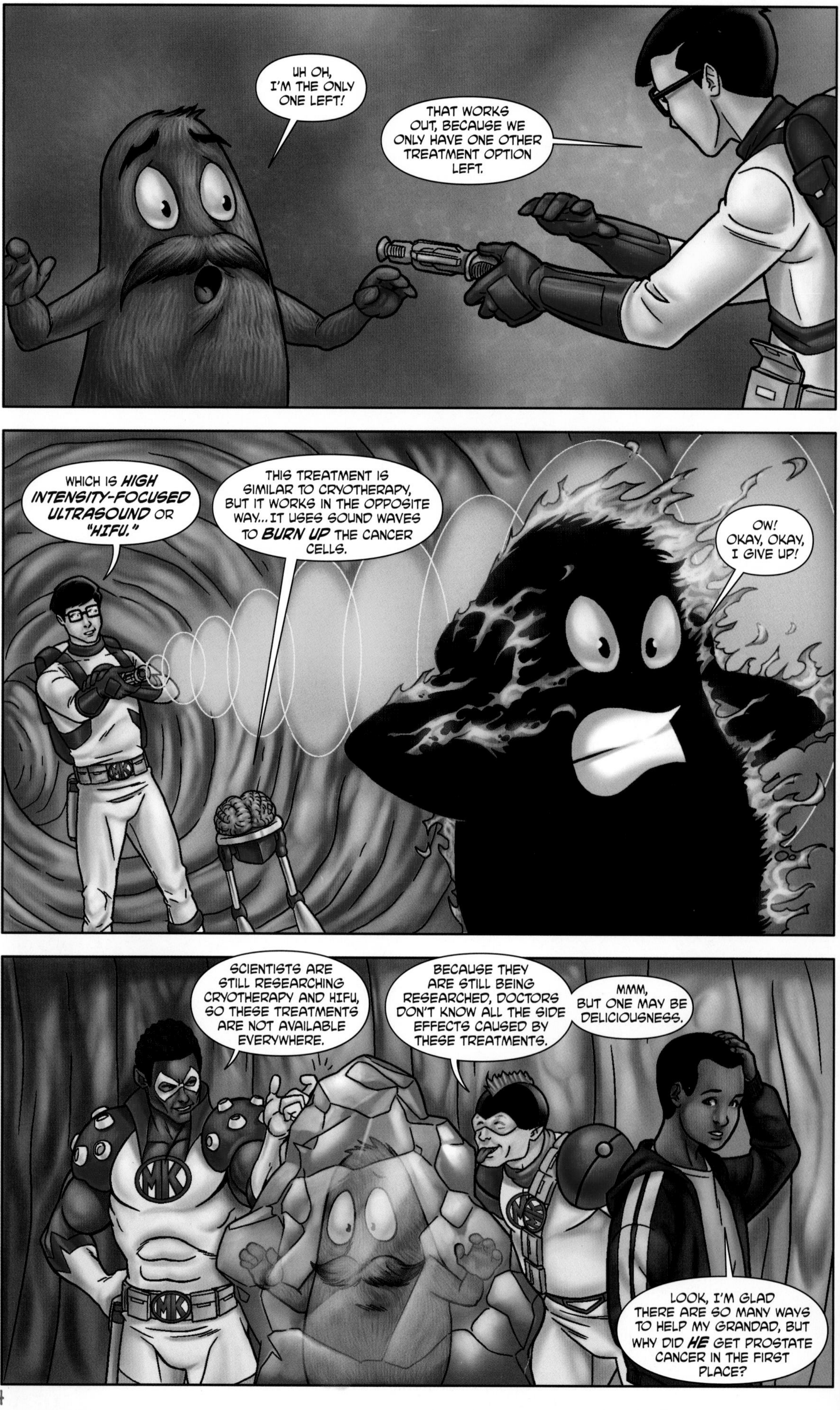
UH OH, I'M THE ONLY ONE LEFT!
THAT WORKS OUT, BECAUSE WE ONLY HAVE ONE OTHER TREATMENT OPTION LEFT.
WHICH IS HIGH INTENSITY-FOCUSED ULTRASOUND OR "HIFU."
THIS TREATMENT IS SIMILAR TO CRYOTHERAPY, BUT IT WORKS IN THE OPPOSITE WAY... IT USES SOUND WAVES TO BURN UP THE CANCER CELLS.
OW! OKAY, OKAY, I GIVE UP!
SCIENTISTS ARE STILL RESEARCHING CRYOTHERAPY AND HIFU, SO THESE TREATMENTS ARE NOT AVAILABLE EVERYWHERE.
BECAUSE THEY ARE STILL BEING RESEARCHED, DOCTORS DON'T KNOW ALL THE SIDE EFFECTS CAUSED BY THESE TREATMENTS.
MMM, BUT ONE MAY BE DELICIOUSNESS.
LOOK, I'M GLAD THERE ARE SO MANY WAYS TO HELP MY GRANDAD, BUT WHY DID HE GET PROSTATE CANCER IN THE FIRST PLACE?

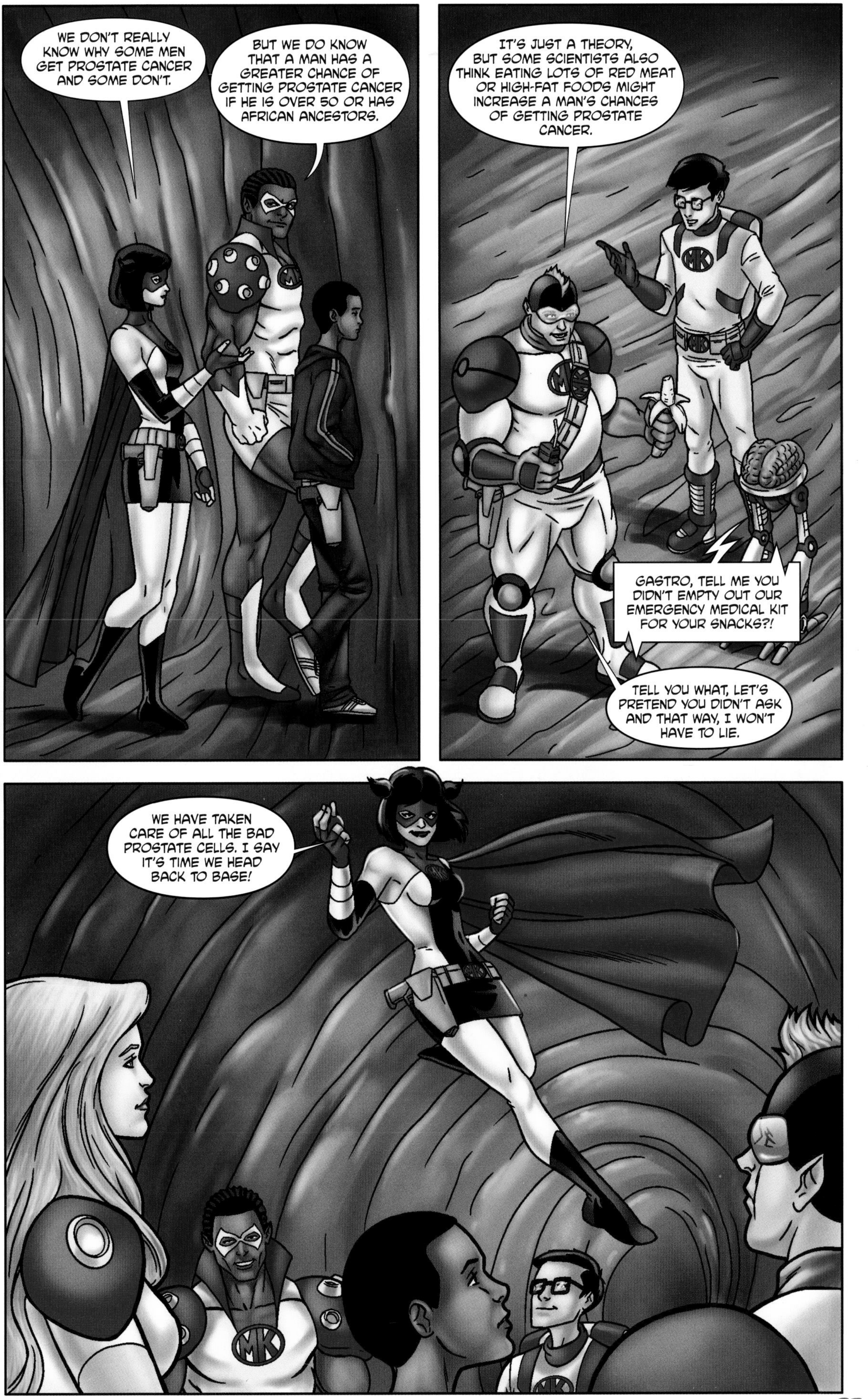
WE DON'T REALLY KNOW WHY SOME MEN GET PROSTATE CANCER AND SOME DON'T.
BUT WE DO KNOW THAT A MAN HAS A GREATER CHANCE OF GETTING PROSTATE CANCER IF HE IS OVER 50 OR HAS AFRICAN ANCESTORS.
IT'S JUST A THEORY, BUT SOME SCIENTISTS ALSO THINK EATING LOTS OF RED MEAT OR HIGH-FAT FOODS MIGHT INCREASE A MAN'S CHANCES OF GETTING PROSTATE CANCER.
GASTRO, TELL ME YOU DIDN'T EMPTY OUT OUR EMERGENCY MEDICAL KIT FOR YOUR SNACKS?!
TELL YOU WHAT, LET'S PRETEND YOU DIDN'T ASK AND THAT WAY, I WON'T HAVE TO LIE.
WE HAVE TAKEN CARE OF ALL THE BAD PROSTATE CELLS. I SAY IT'S TIME WE HEAD BACK TO BASE!

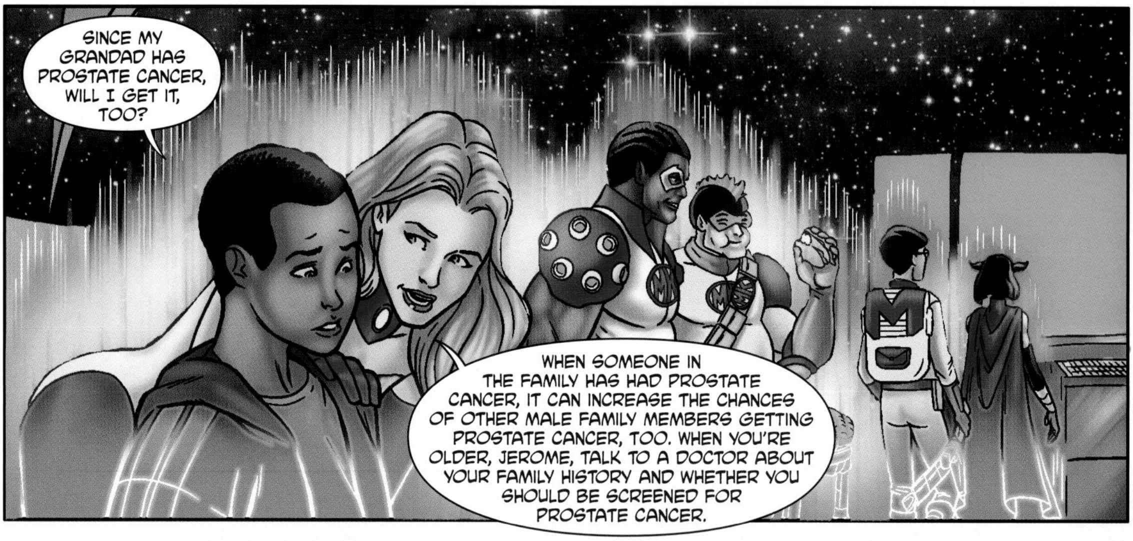
SINCE MY GRANDAD HAS PROSTATE CANCER, WILL I GET IT, TOO?
WHEN SOMEONE IN THE FAMILY HAS HAD PROSTATE CANCER, IT CAN INCREASE THE CHANCES OF OTHER MALE FAMILY MEMBERS GETTING PROSTATE CANCER, TOO. WHEN YOU'RE OLDER, JEROME, TALK TO A DOCTOR ABOUT YOUR FAMILY HISTORY AND WHETHER YOU SHOULD BE SCREENED FOR PROSTATE CANCER.

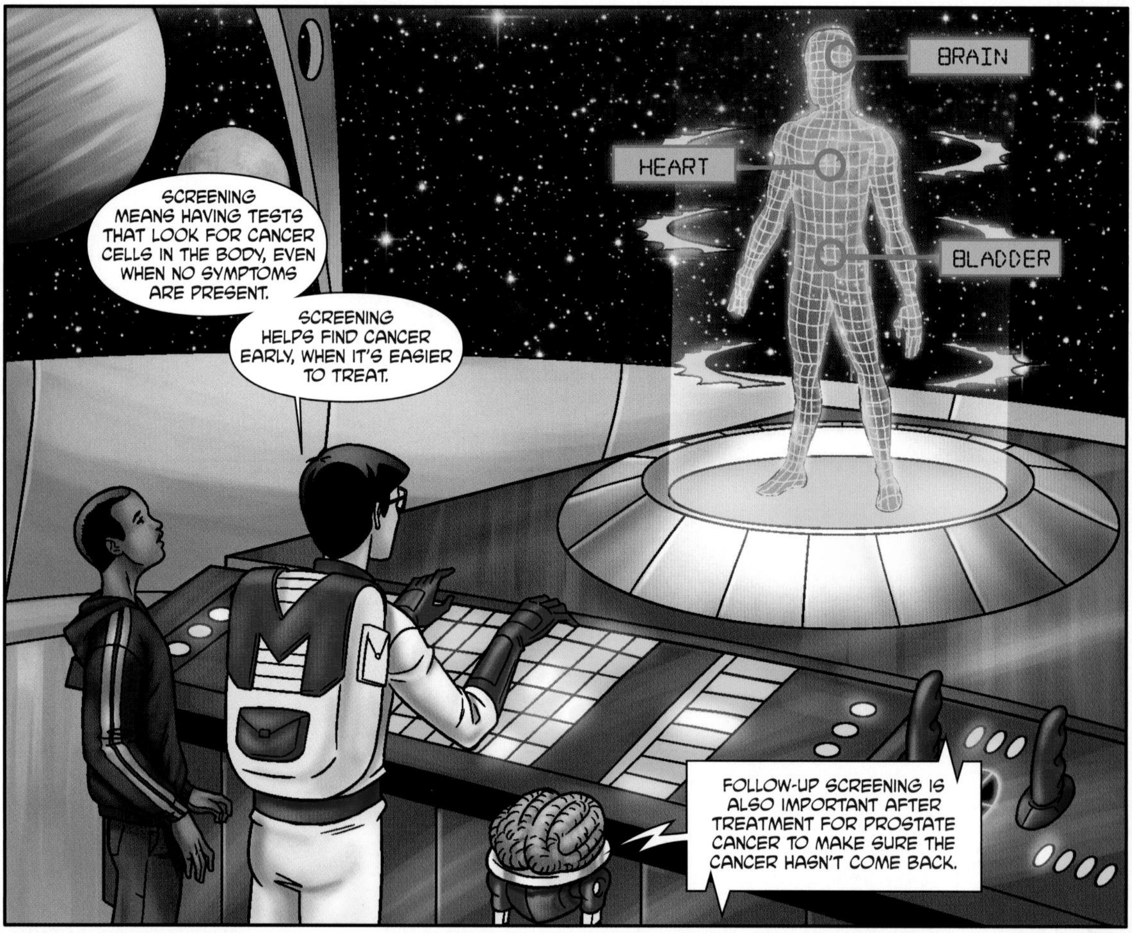
BRAIN
HEART
BLADDER
SCREENING MEANS HAVING TESTS THAT LOOK FOR CANCER CELLS IN THE BODY, EVEN WHEN NO SYMPTOMS ARE PRESENT.
SCREENING HELPS FIND CANCER EARLY, WHEN IT'S EASIER TO TREAT.
FOLLOW-UP SCREENING IS ALSO IMPORTANT AFTER TREATMENT FOR PROSTATE CANCER TO MAKE SURE THE CANCER HASN'T COME BACK.

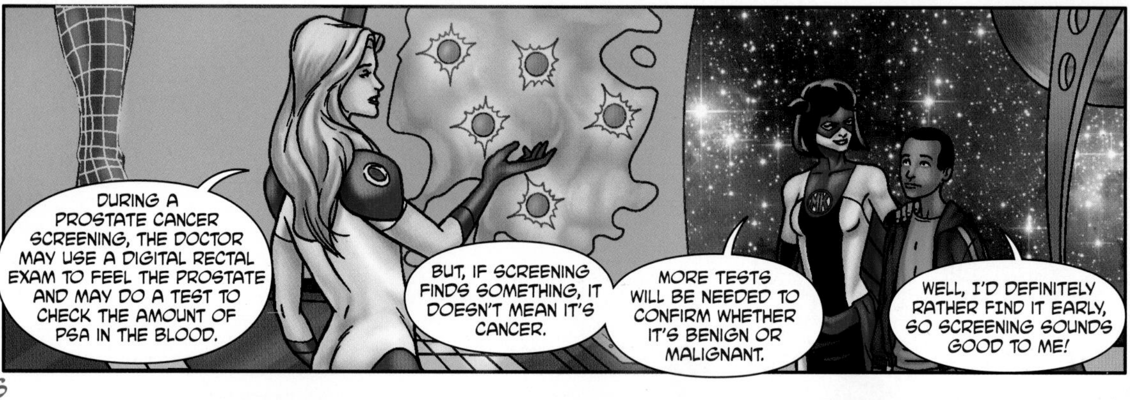
DURING A PROSTATE CANCER SCREENING, THE DOCTOR MAY USE A DIGITAL RECTAL EXAM TO FEEL THE PROSTATE AND MAY DO A TEST TO CHECK THE AMOUNT OF PSA IN THE BLOOD.
BUT, IF SCREENING FINDS SOMETHING, IT DOESN'T MEAN IT'S CANCER.
MORE TESTS WILL BE NEEDED TO CONFIRM WHETHER IT'S BENIGN OR MALIGNANT.
WELL, I'D DEFINITELY RATHER FIND IT EARLY, SO SCREENING SOUNDS GOOD TO ME!

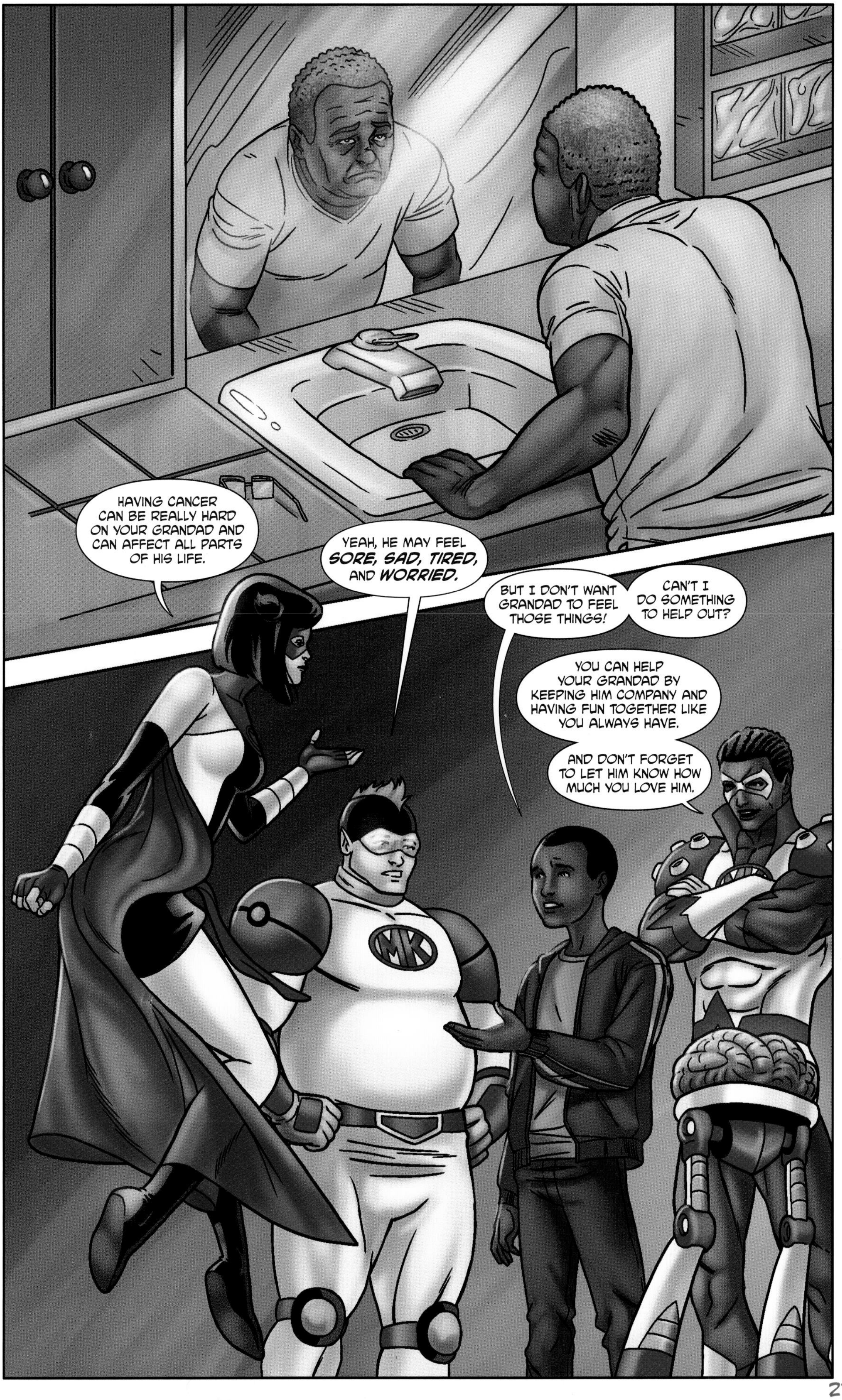
HAVING CANCER CAN BE REALLY HARD ON YOUR GRANDAD AND CAN AFFECT ALL PARTS OF HIS LIFE.
YEAH, HE MAY FEEL *SORE, SAD, TIRED,* AND *WORRIED.*
BUT I DON'T WANT GRANDAD TO FEEL THOSE THINGS!
CAN'T I DO SOMETHING TO HELP OUT?
YOU CAN HELP YOUR GRANDAD BY KEEPING HIM COMPANY AND HAVING FUN TOGETHER LIKE YOU ALWAYS HAVE.
AND DON'T FORGET TO LET HIM KNOW HOW MUCH YOU LOVE HIM.
MK

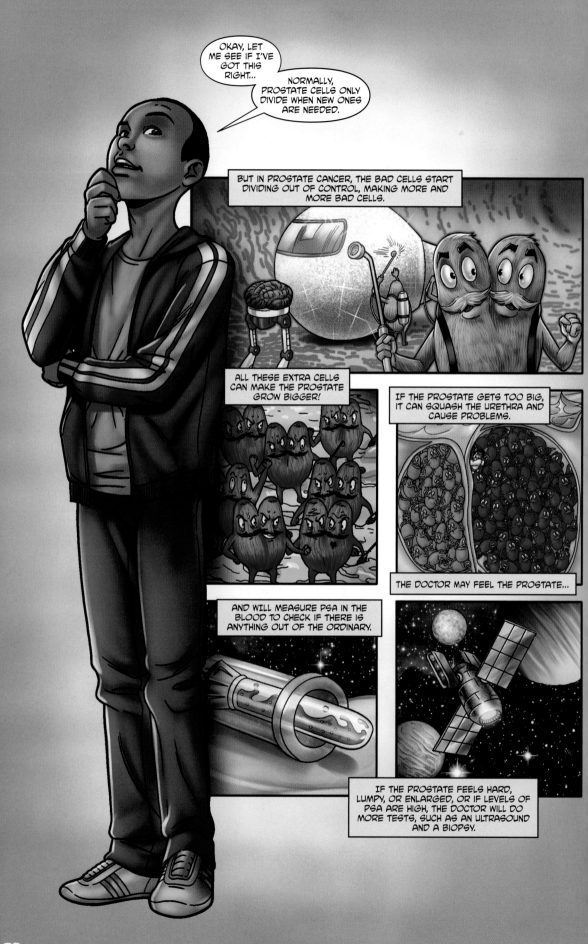

OKAY, LET ME SEE IF I'VE GOT THIS RIGHT...

NORMALLY, PROSTATE CELLS ONLY DIVIDE WHEN NEW ONES ARE NEEDED.

BUT IN PROSTATE CANCER, THE BAD CELLS START DIVIDING OUT OF CONTROL, MAKING MORE AND MORE BAD CELLS.

ALL THESE EXTRA CELLS CAN MAKE THE PROSTATE GROW BIGGER!

IF THE PROSTATE GETS TOO BIG, IT CAN SQUASH THE URETHRA AND CAUSE PROBLEMS.

THE DOCTOR MAY FEEL THE PROSTATE...

AND WILL MEASURE PSA IN THE BLOOD TO CHECK IF THERE IS ANYTHING OUT OF THE ORDINARY.

IF THE PROSTATE FEELS HARD, LUMPY, OR ENLARGED, OR IF LEVELS OF PSA ARE HIGH, THE DOCTOR WILL DO MORE TESTS, SUCH AS AN ULTRASOUND AND A BIOPSY.

THE BIOPSY WILL SHOW WHETHER THE CELLS ARE *BENIGN (NOT CANCER)*...

OR *MALIGNANT (CANCER)*.

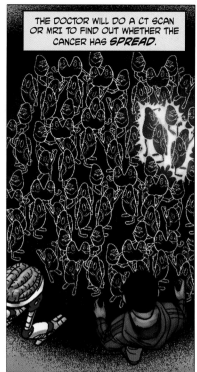

THE DOCTOR WILL DO A CT SCAN OR MRI TO FIND OUT WHETHER THE CANCER HAS *SPREAD*.

THESE TESTS WILL HELP THE DOCTOR DETERMINE THE BEST TREATMENT OPTIONS FOR MY GRANDAD.

HIS TREATMENT OPTIONS MAY INCLUDE WAITING AND WATCHING, SURGERY, RADIATION THERAPY, HORMONE THERAPY, CHEMOTHERAPY, CRYOTHERAPY, OR HIFU.

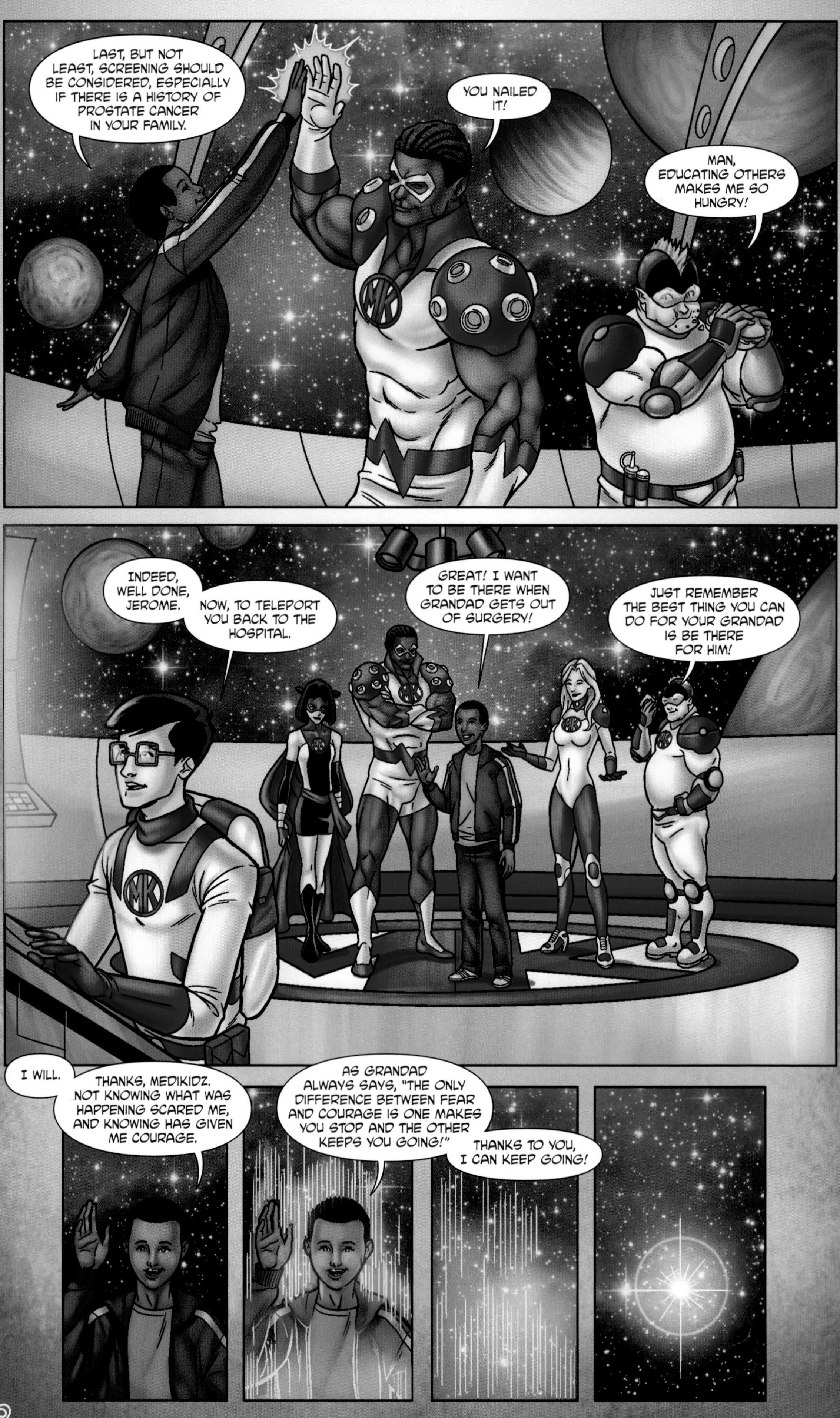
LAST, BUT NOT LEAST, SCREENING SHOULD BE CONSIDERED, ESPECIALLY IF THERE IS A HISTORY OF PROSTATE CANCER IN YOUR FAMILY.
YOU NAILED IT!
MAN, EDUCATING OTHERS MAKES ME SO HUNGRY!
INDEED, WELL DONE, JEROME.
NOW, TO TELEPORT YOU BACK TO THE HOSPITAL.
GREAT! I WANT TO BE THERE WHEN GRANDAD GETS OUT OF SURGERY!
JUST REMEMBER THE BEST THING YOU CAN DO FOR YOUR GRANDAD IS BE THERE FOR HIM!
I WILL.
THANKS, MEDIKIDZ. NOT KNOWING WHAT WAS HAPPENING SCARED ME, AND KNOWING HAS GIVEN ME COURAGE.
AS GRANDAD ALWAYS SAYS, "THE ONLY DIFFERENCE BETWEEN FEAR AND COURAGE IS ONE MAKES YOU STOP AND THE OTHER KEEPS YOU GOING!"
THANKS TO YOU, I CAN KEEP GOING!

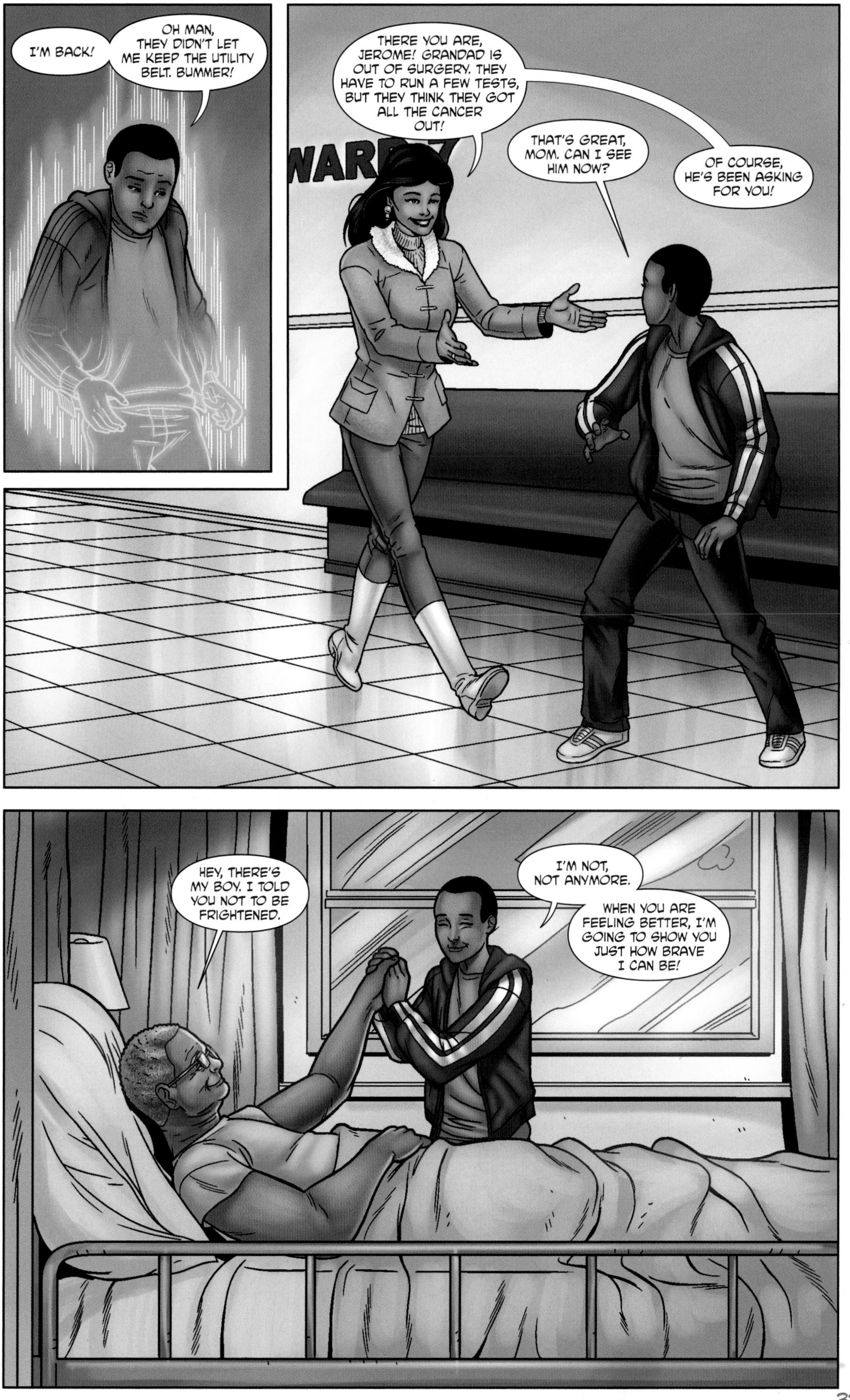
I'M BACK!
OH MAN, THEY DIDN'T LET ME KEEP THE UTILITY BELT. BUMMER!
THERE YOU ARE, JEROME! GRANDAD IS OUT OF SURGERY. THEY HAVE TO RUN A FEW TESTS, BUT THEY THINK THEY GOT ALL THE CANCER OUT!
THAT'S GREAT, MOM. CAN I SEE HIM NOW?
OF COURSE, HE'S BEEN ASKING FOR YOU!
HEY, THERE'S MY BOY. I TOLD YOU NOT TO BE FRIGHTENED.
I'M NOT, NOT ANYMORE.
WHEN YOU ARE FEELING BETTER, I'M GOING TO SHOW YOU JUST HOW BRAVE I CAN BE!

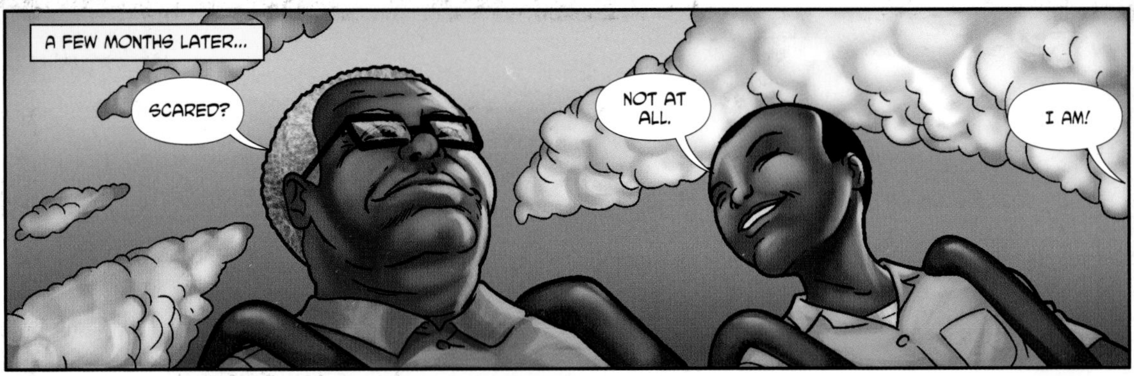
A FEW MONTHS LATER...
SCARED?
NOT AT ALL.
I AM!

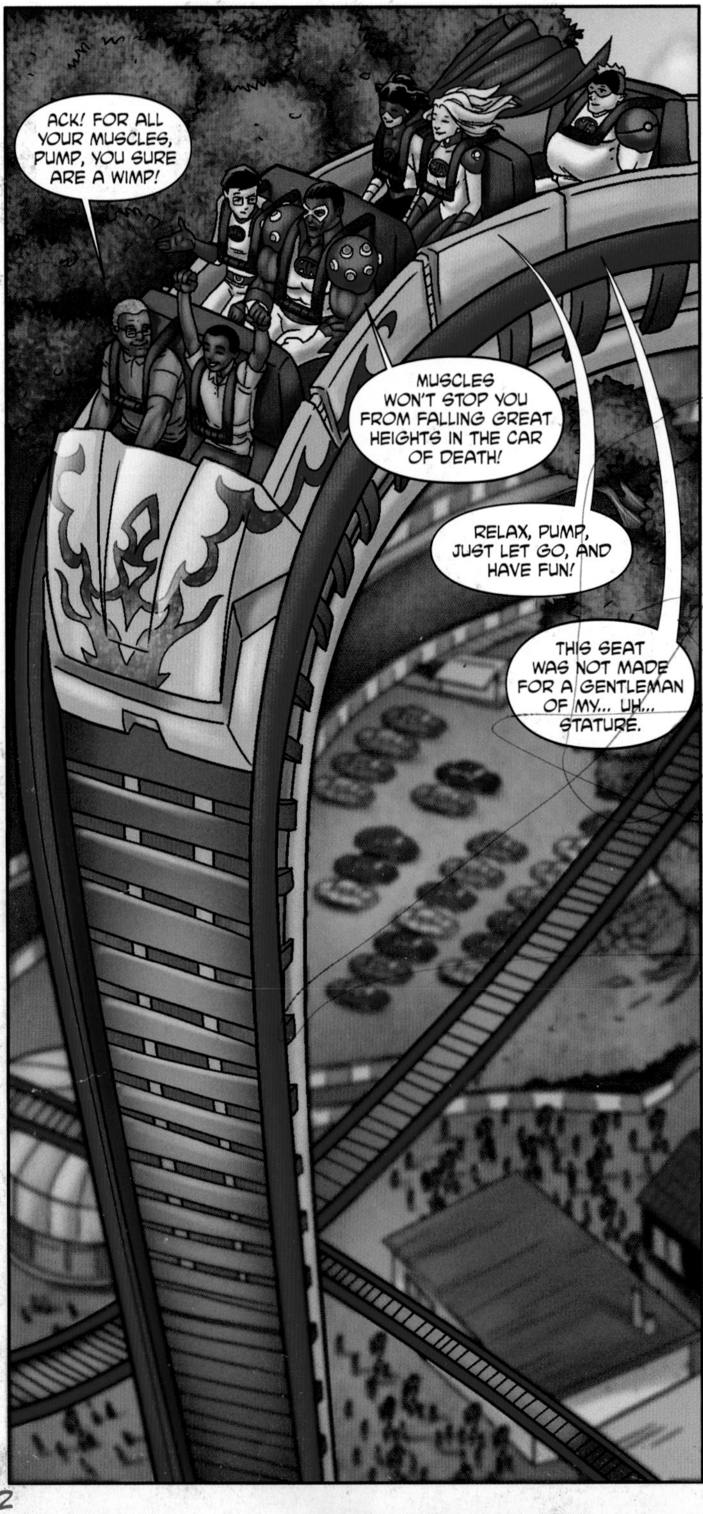
ACK! FOR ALL YOUR MUSCLES, PUMP, YOU SURE ARE A WIMP!
MUSCLES WON'T STOP YOU FROM FALLING GREAT HEIGHTS IN THE CAR OF DEATH!
RELAX, PUMP, JUST LET GO, AND HAVE FUN!
THIS SEAT WAS NOT MADE FOR A GENTLEMAN OF MY... UH... STATURE.

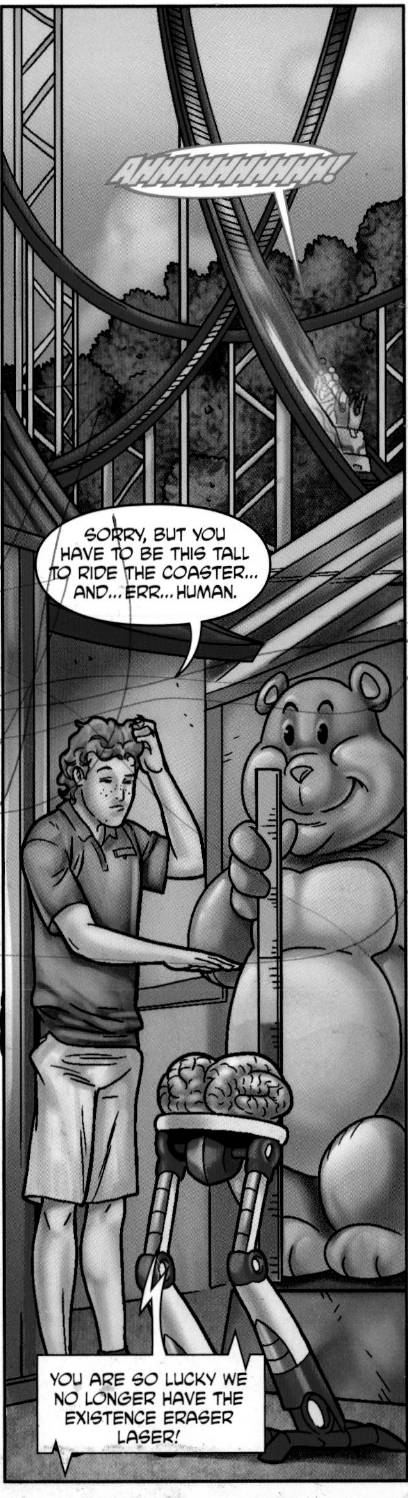
AHHHHHHHHHH!
SORRY, BUT YOU HAVE TO BE THIS TALL TO RIDE THE COASTER... AND... ERR... HUMAN.
YOU ARE SO LUCKY WE NO LONGER HAVE THE EXISTENCE ERASER LASER!